# Using this atlas

## How to use this atlas

The atlas is in five colour coded sections. These are shown on the **List of contents** on the page opposite.

There are two ways to find information in this atlas.

- Firstly, if you are looking for a particular topic, look for it on the **List of contents** on the page opposite or on the **Subject list** on this page. For example, maps showing Energy resources can be found on pages 15 and 41.

- Secondly, if you are looking for a particular place or feature, look for the name of the place in the **Index of place names** on pages 64–65. You can refer to page 63 **Finding places** to help you find the place on the map. If you know roughly where a particular name occurs, you can use the **Key map of the continents** below or the **List of contents** to find the map page number and then look for it on the map.

## Subject list

| | | |
|---|---|---|
| Airports | **17, 43** | |
| Airways | **43** | |
| Biofuels | **15** | |
| Carbon dioxide | **34** | |
| Cardinal points | **5** | |
| Cars | **16** | |
| Channel Tunnel | **17** | |
| Climate | **8, 32** | |
| Climate graphs | **8, 32** | |
| Coal | **15, 41** | |
| Commonwealth | **23** | |
| Compass | **5** | |
| Coniferous forest | **36** | |
| Conservation | **13** | |
| Counties | **19** | |
| Deciduous forest | **36** | |
| Desert | **36** | |
| Development aid | **45** | |
| Direction | **5** | |
| Distance table | **16, 43** | |
| Earth | **28** | |
| Earthquakes | **39** | |
| Energy resources | **15, 41** | |
| Equator | **63** | |
| European Union | **23** | |
| Famine | **45** | |
| Farming | **12, 40** | |
| Ferry ports | **17** | |
| Fishing | **12, 40** | |
| Flooding | **11** | |
| Food | **12, 45** | |
| Geothermal power | **41** | |
| Global warming | **34** | |
| Green Belt areas | **13** | |
| Greenhouse effect | **34** | |
| Hydroelectricity | **15, 41** | |
| Income | **14, 44** | |
| Land use | **40** | |
| Latitude | **63** | |
| Life expectancy | **44** | |
| Longitude | **63** | |
| Magnetic Pole | **5** | |
| Manufacturing | **14** | |
| Moon | **29** | |
| National parks | **13** | |
| Natural gas | **15, 41** | |
| Non-renewable energy | **41** | |
| Nuclear energy | **15** | |
| Oil | **15, 41** | |
| Old people | **20** | |
| Panama Canal | **42** | |
| Plate boundaries | **38** | |
| Population change | **47** | |
| Population density | **20** | |
| Population growth | **46** | |
| Ports | **17, 42** | |
| Prime Meridian | **63** | |
| Railways | **17** | |
| Rainfall | **8, 33** | |
| Reading and writing | **45** | |
| Regions | **18** | |
| Renewable energy | **15, 41** | |
| Reservoirs | **10** | |
| Rising sea levels | **35** | |
| River pollution | **10** | |
| Rivers | **6, 30** | |
| Roads | **16** | |
| Rock types | **6** | |
| Savanna | **36** | |
| Scale | **4** | |
| Seasons | **29** | |
| Service industries | **14** | |
| Shipping routes | **42** | |
| Snowfall | **9** | |
| Solar power | **41** | |
| Solar system | **28** | |
| Steppe | **36** | |
| Suez Canal | **42** | |
| Sunshine | **9** | |
| Temperature | **9, 33** | |
| Temperature change | **35** | |
| Tidal power | **41** | |
| Tourism | **22, 43** | |
| Tropical rainforest | **36** | |
| Tsunami | **39** | |
| Tundra | **36** | |
| Types of farm | **12** | |
| Unemployment | **14** | |
| Unitary authorities | **19** | |
| United Nations | **23** | |
| Urban population | **47** | |
| Volcanoes | **38** | |
| Water cycle | **11** | |
| Wave power | **41** | |
| Weather | **8** | |
| Wind | **9** | |
| Wind power | **15, 41** | |
| Workforce | **14** | |
| Young people | **20** | |

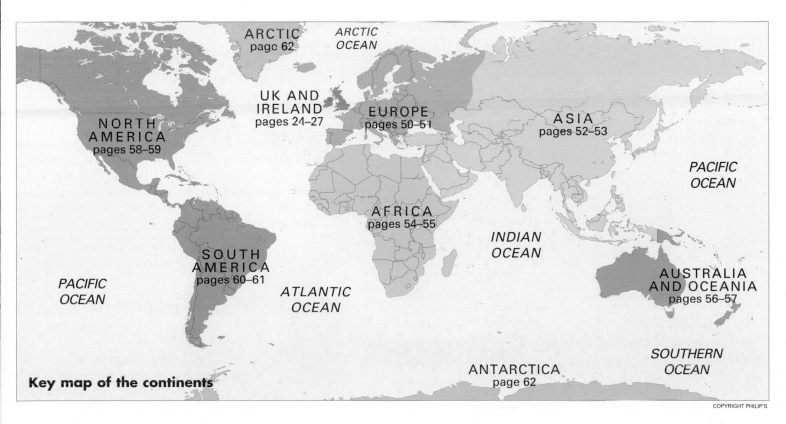

**Key map of the continents**

ARCTIC page 62

ARCTIC OCEAN

UK AND IRELAND pages 24–27

EUROPE pages 50–51

ASIA pages 52–53

NORTH AMERICA pages 58–59

PACIFIC OCEAN

AFRICA pages 54–55

INDIAN OCEAN

SOUTH AMERICA pages 60–61

PACIFIC OCEAN

ATLANTIC OCEAN

AUSTRALIA AND OCEANIA pages 56–57

ANTARCTICA page 62

SOUTHERN OCEAN

# What is a map?

These small maps explain the meaning of some of the lines and colours on the atlas maps.

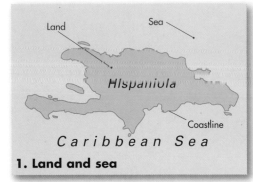

**1. Land and sea**

This is how an island is shown on a map. The land is coloured green and the sea is blue. The coastline is a blue line.

**2. Rivers and lakes**

There are some lakes on the island and rivers that flow down to the sea.

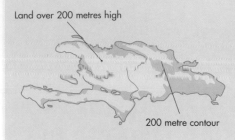

**3. Height of the land – 1**

This map shows the land over 200 metres high in a lighter colour. The height of the land is shown by contour lines and layer colours.

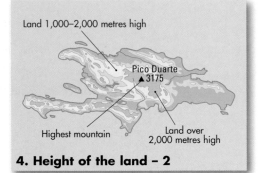

**4. Height of the land – 2**

This map shows more contour lines and layer colours. It shows that the highest mountain is in the centre of the island and that it is over 3,000 metres high.

**5. Countries**

This is a way of showing different information about the island. It shows that the island is divided into two countries. They are separated by a country boundary.

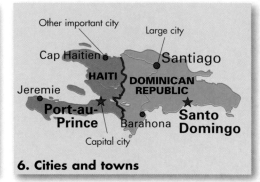

**6. Cities and towns**

There are cities and towns on the island. The two capital cities are shown with a special symbol. Other large or important cities are shown by a red circle.

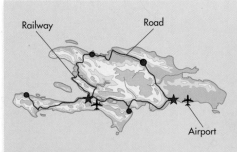

**7. Transport information**

This map shows the most important roads, railways and airports. Transport routes connect the cities and towns.

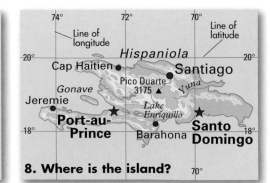

**8. Where is the island?**

This map gives lines of latitude and longitude and shows where the island is in the world. Page 59 in the atlas shows the same island on a map at a different scale.

**9. A complete map**

This map is using the country colouring and showing the letter-figure codes used in the index.

# Map information

## Symbols

Page 17

A map symbol shows the position of something – for example, circles for towns or an aeroplane for an airport.

Page 46

On some maps a dot or a symbol stands for a large number – for example, 500,000 people or cities with over 10 million people.

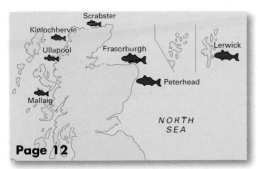

Page 12

The size of the symbol can be bigger or smaller, to show different numbers. The symbol here shows fishing ports in the UK.

## Colours

Page 51

Colours are used on some maps so that separate areas, such as countries, as in this map, can be seen clearly.

Page 36

Patterns on maps often spread across country borders. This map shows different types of vegetation in the world.

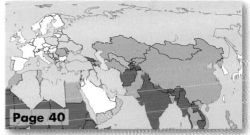

Page 8

On other maps, areas that are the same in some way have the same colour to show patterns. This map shows rainfall.

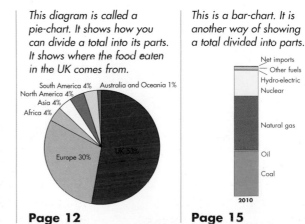

Page 40

Colours that are lighter or darker are used on some maps to show less or more of something. This map shows farming.

## Graphs and charts

Graphs and charts are used to give more information about subjects shown on the maps. A graph shows how something changes over time.

This graph shows the rainfall for each month in a year as a blue bar that can be measured on the scale at the side of the graph.

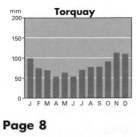

Page 8

This diagram is called a pie-chart. It shows how you can divide a total into its parts. It shows where the food eaten in the UK comes from.

Page 12

This is a bar-chart. It is another way of showing a total divided into parts.

Page 15

# Scale

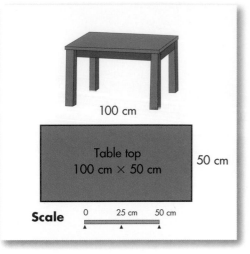

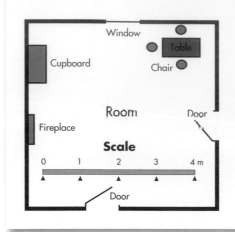

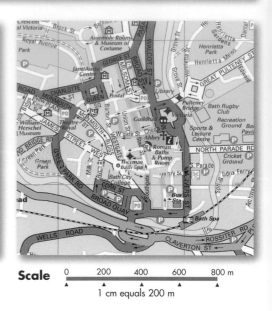

This is a drawing of the top of a table, looking down on it. It is 100 cm long and 50 cm wide. The drawing measures 4 × 2 cm. It is drawn to scale: 1 cm on the drawing equals 25 cm on the table.

This is a plan of a room looking down from above. 1 cm on the plan equals 1 metre in the room. The same table is shown, but now at a smaller scale. Use the scale bar to find the measurements of other parts of the room.

This is a map of an area in the city of Bath. Large buildings can be seen but other buildings are too small to show. Below are atlas maps of different scales.

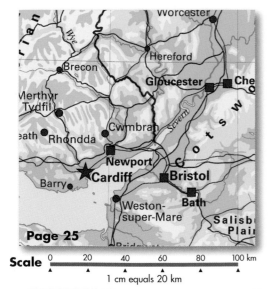

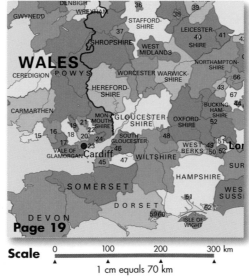

### Scale bars

This distance represents 1 mile

This distance represents 1 kilometre

These examples of scale bars are at the scale of 1 cm equals 0.5 km

Signposts still have miles on them. 1 mile = 1.6 km, or 10 miles is the same as 16 kilometres.
On the maps of the UK and Ireland and the continents kilometre scale bars are used. On the maps of the continents, where you cannot see the UK and Ireland, a small map is shown to give you some idea of size and scale.

UK & IRELAND
On same scale

# Direction

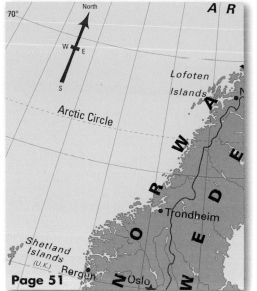

Page 51

## The Cardinal Points

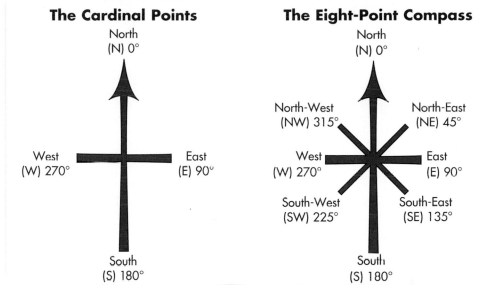

North
(N) 0°

West
(W) 270°

East
(E) 90°

South
(S) 180°

## The Eight-Point Compass

North
(N) 0°

North-West
(NW) 315°

North-East
(NE) 45°

West
(W) 270°

East
(E) 90°

South-West
(SW) 225°

South-East
(SE) 135°

South
(S) 180°

Many of the maps in this atlas have a North Point showing the direction of north. It points in the same direction as the lines of longitude. The four main directions shown are called the cardinal points.

Direction is measured in degrees. This diagram shows the degree numbers for each cardinal point. The direction is measured clockwise from north. The diagram on the right shows all the points of the compass and the divisions between the cardinal points. For example, between north and east there is north-east, between south and west is south-west. You can work out the cardinal points at your home by looking for the sun rising in the east and setting in the west.

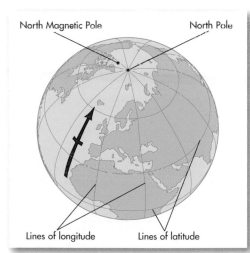

North Magnetic Pole

North Pole

Lines of longitude

Lines of latitude

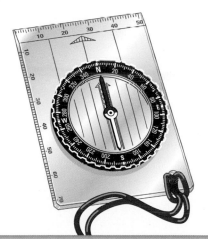

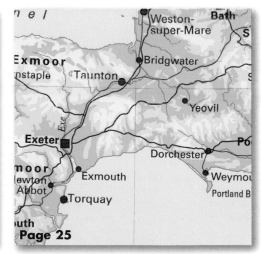

Page 25

The Earth has a spot near the North Pole that is called the Magnetic Pole. If a piece of metal that was magnetized at one end was left to float, then the magnetized tip would point to the North Magnetic Pole.

The needle of a compass is magnetized and it always points north. If you know where you are and want to go to another place, you can measure your direction from a map and use a compass to guide you.

North is at the top of this map. Look at the points of the compass on the diagram above and the positions of places on the map. Taunton is north-east of Exeter and Dorchester is south-east of Taunton.

5

# Rocks, mountains and rivers

## Rocks

This map shows the different types of rock in Great Britain and Ireland.

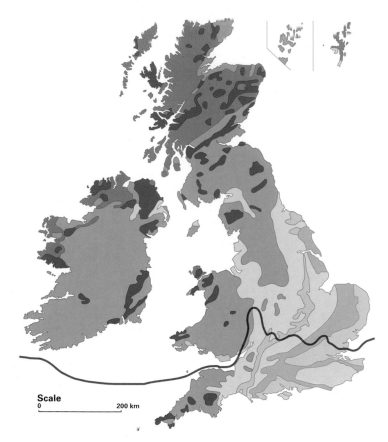

**Scale**
0       200 km

### Type of rock

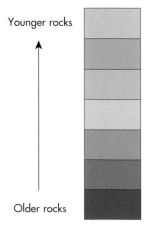

Younger rocks

Older rocks

Young sand, clay and river mud

Chalk

Young limestone

Sandstone and clay

Old hard rocks, old limestone, grit, coal, slate, shale and old sandstone

Very old hard rocks

Old volcanoes, granite and basalt

Glaciers came as far south as this line up to 10,000 years ago

### Longest rivers

(length in kilometres)

1. Shannon .................... 370
2. Severn ..................... 354
3. Thames .................... 335
4. Trent ...................... 297
5. Aire ....................... 259
6. Great Ouse ............... 230
7. Wye ....................... 215
8. Tay ........................ 188
9. Nene ...................... 161
10. Clyde ..................... 158

*The longest river in Northern Ireland is the River Bann (129 kilometres). The longest river completely in Wales is the Tywi (109 kilometres).*

### Largest lakes

(area in square kilometres)

1. Lough Neagh ..................... 382
2. Lough Corrib .................... 168
3. Lough Derg ..................... 120
4. Lower Lough Erne .............. 105
5. Loch Lomond ................... 71
6. Loch Ness ...................... 57

*The largest lake in England is Windermere (15 square kilometres). The largest lake in Wales is Llyn Vyrnwy (8 square kilometres).*

### Largest islands

(area in square kilometres)

1. Great Britain .............. 229,880
2. Ireland .................... 84,400
3. Lewis and Harris .......... 2,225
4. Skye ....................... 1,666
5. Shetland (Mainland) ...... 967
6. Mull ....................... 899
7. Anglesey .................. 714
8. Islay ...................... 615
9. Isle of Man ............... 572
10. Isle of Wight .............. 381

### Highest mountains

(height in metres)

In Scotland:
  Ben Nevis .......................... 1,344
In Wales:
  Snowdon ........................... 1,085
In Ireland:
  Carrauntoohill ................... 1,041
In England:
  Scafell Pike ....................... 978
In Northern Ireland:
  Slieve Donard ..................... 852

**Scale**
0       200 km

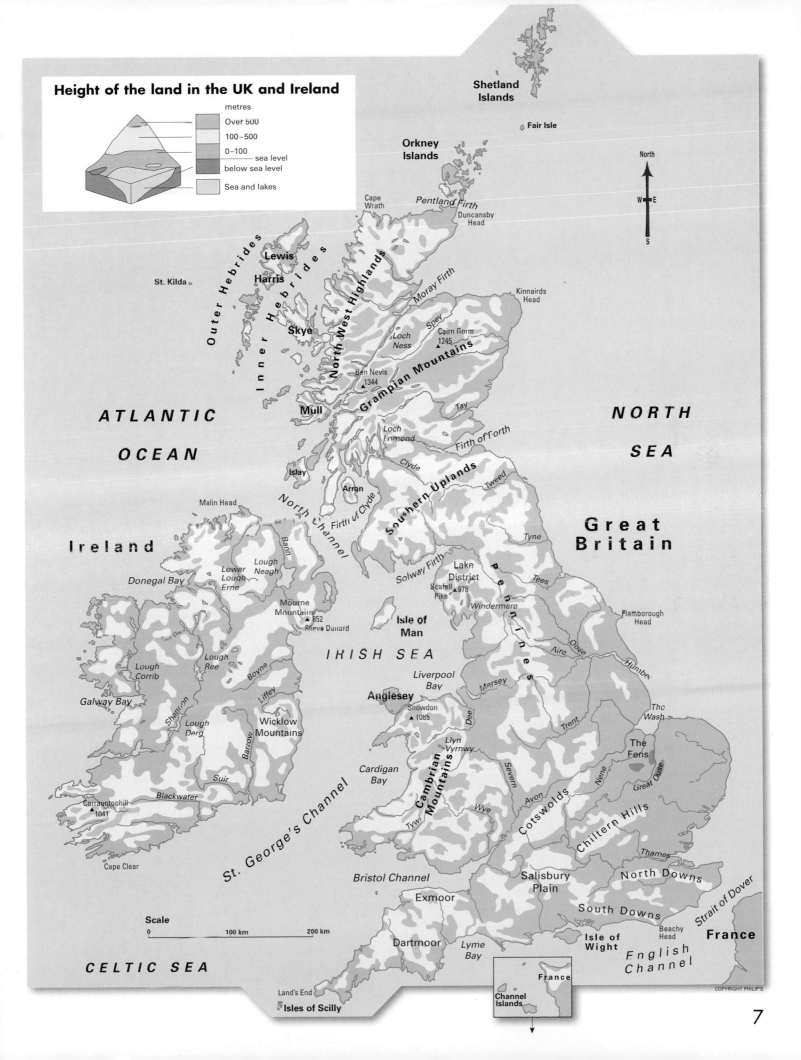

## Height of the land in the UK and Ireland

metres
- Over 500
- 100–500
- 0–100 — sea level
- below sea level
- Sea and lakes

**Shetland Islands**

Fair Isle

**Orkney Islands**

Cape Wrath

*Pentland Firth*

Duncansby Head

St. Kilda

**Lewis**

**Harris**

**Outer Hebrides**

**Inner Hebrides**

*North West Highlands*

*Moray Firth*

Kinnairds Head

**Skye**

*Spey*

*Loch Ness*

Cairn Gorm ▲ 1245

**Grampian Mountains**

Ben Nevis ▲ 1344

**Mull**

*Tay*

*Loch Lomond*

*Firth of Forth*

Islay

*Clyde*

**Arran**

*Firth of Clyde*

**Southern Uplands**

*Tweed*

North

W ■ E

S

**ATLANTIC OCEAN**

**NORTH SEA**

Malin Head

**North Channel**

*Tyne*

**Great Britain**

**Ireland**

*Bann*

Lower Lough Erne

*Lough Neagh*

Donegal Bay

*Solway Firth*

**Lake District**

Scafell Pike ▲ 978

*P e n n i n e s*

*Tees*

Mourne Mountains ▲ 852

Slieve Donard

*Windermere*

Flamborough Head

**Isle of Man**

**IRISH SEA**

Lough Corrib

Lough Ree

*Boyne*

*Shannon*

*Liverpool Bay*

*Aire*

*Ouse*

*Humber*

Galway Bay

*Liffey*

**Anglesey**

*Marsey*

*Mersey*

*Trent*

The Wash

Lough Derg

*Barrow*

**Wicklow Mountains**

Snowdon ▲ 1085

*Dee*

**The Fens**

*Suir*

**Cardigan Bay**

Llyn Vyrnwy

**Cambrian Mountains**

*Severn*

*Avon*

*Nene*

*Great Ouse*

Carrauntoohill ▲ 1041

*Blackwater*

*Tywi*

*Wye*

**Cotswolds**

**Chiltern Hills**

*Thames*

Cape Clear

**St. George's Channel**

**Bristol Channel**

**Salisbury Plain**

**North Downs**

**Exmoor**

**South Downs**

Beachy Head

Strait of Dover

**Isle of Wight**

**France**

**Dartmoor**

Lyme Bay

*English Channel*

**CELTIC SEA**

Land's End

**Isles of Scilly**

France

Channel Islands

Scale

0      100 km      200 km

COPYRIGHT PHILIP'S

# Weather and climate

Rainfall is measured at many places every day. Each year, all the measurements are put together and graphs are made, like the ones shown on this page. Experts in the weather use these measurements to find out the average amount of rainfall for each place and for each year. They can then show this on climate maps, like the map below. Graphs and maps are also made for average temperatures and other types of weather (see opposite page). These help the experts to see patterns in the weather over a long period of time. These patterns in the weather show a country's climate. The maps on these pages show you the climate of the UK and Ireland.

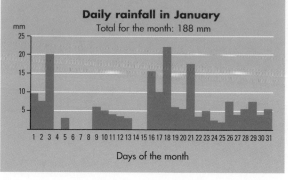

If you collect the rainfall each day and measure it, then you could draw a graph like this.

**Daily rainfall in January**
Total for the month: 188 mm

Days of the month

## Rainfall

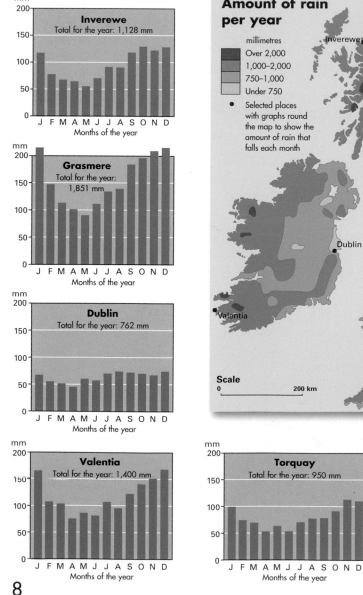

Inverewe
Total for the year: 1,128 mm
Months of the year

Grasmere
Total for the year: 1,851 mm
Months of the year

Dublin
Total for the year: 762 mm
Months of the year

Valentia
Total for the year: 1,400 mm
Months of the year

Torquay
Total for the year: 950 mm
Months of the year

Birmingham
Total for the year: 764 mm
Months of the year

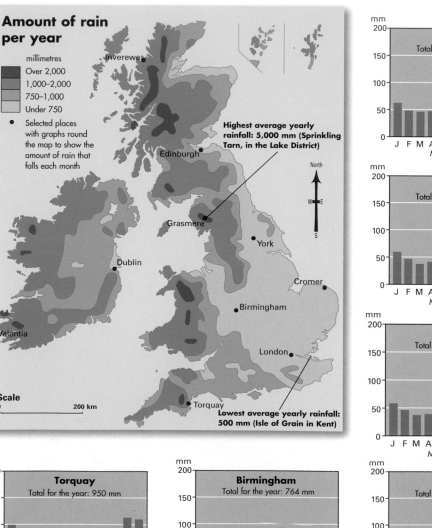

**Amount of rain per year**

millimetres
- Over 2,000
- 1,000–2,000
- 750–1,000
- Under 750

• Selected places with graphs round the map to show the amount of rain that falls each month

Inverewe

Edinburgh

Highest average yearly rainfall: 5,000 mm (Sprinkling Tarn, in the Lake District)

Grasmere

York

Dublin

Cromer

Birmingham

Valentia

London

Torquay

Lowest average yearly rainfall: 500 mm (Isle of Grain in Kent)

North
W — E
S

Scale
0        200 km

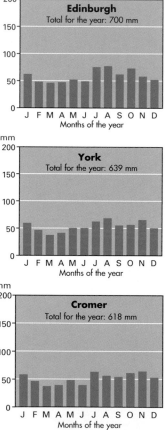

Edinburgh
Total for the year: 700 mm
Months of the year

York
Total for the year: 639 mm
Months of the year

Cromer
Total for the year: 618 mm
Months of the year

London
Total for the year: 593 mm
Months of the year

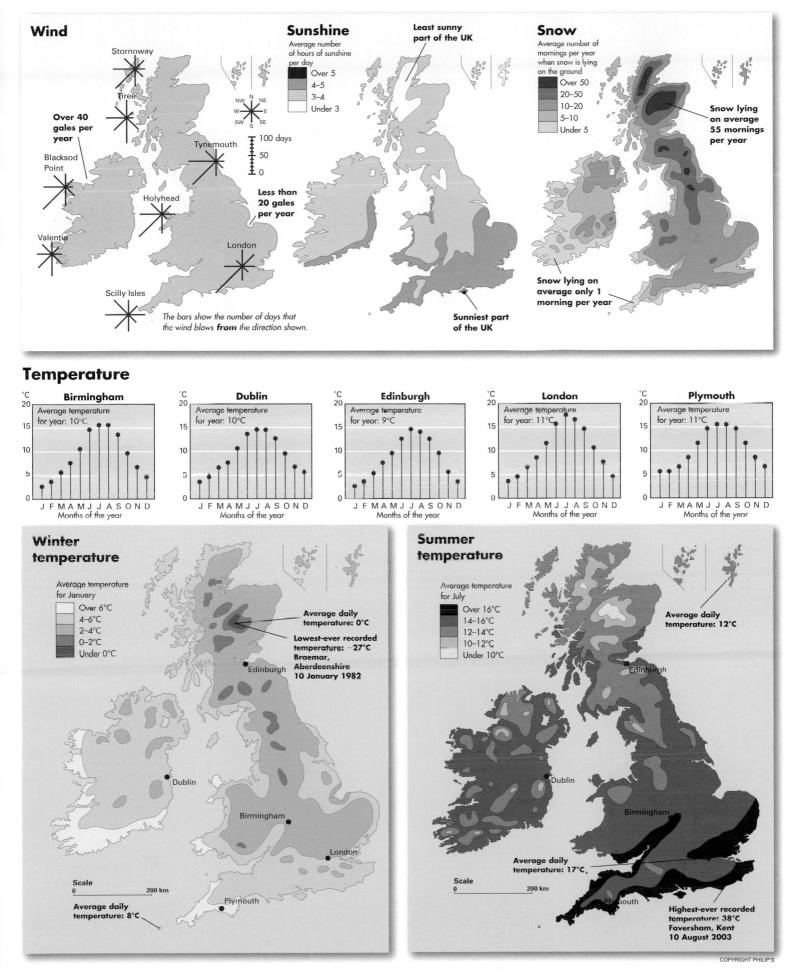

# Wind

Stornoway

Tiree

**Over 40 gales per year**

Blacksod Point

Holyhead

Tynemouth

Valentia

London

Scilly Isles

**Less than 20 gales per year**

NW N NE
W · E
SW S SE

100 days
50
0

*The bars show the number of days that the wind blows **from** the direction shown.*

# Sunshine

Average number of hours of sunshine per day

Over 5
4–5
3–4
Under 3

**Least sunny part of the UK**

**Sunniest part of the UK**

# Snow

Average number of mornings per year when snow is lying on the ground

Over 50
20–50
10–20
5–10
Under 5

**Snow lying on average 55 mornings per year**

**Snow lying on average only 1 morning per year**

# Temperature

### Birmingham
°C
20
15
10
5
0
Average temperature for year: 10°C
J F M A M J J A S O N D
Months of the year

### Dublin
°C
20
15
10
5
0
Average temperature for year: 10°C
J F M A M J J A S O N D
Months of the year

### Edinburgh
°C
20
15
10
5
0
Average temperature for year: 9°C
J F M A M J J A S O N D
Months of the year

### London
°C
20
15
10
5
0
Average temperature for year: 11°C
J F M A M J J A S O N D
Months of the year

### Plymouth
°C
20
15
10
5
0
Average temperature for year: 11°C
J F M A M J J A S O N D
Months of the year

## Winter temperature

Average temperature for January

Over 6°C
4–6°C
2–4°C
0–2°C
Under 0°C

**Average daily temperature: 0°C**

**Lowest-ever recorded temperature: −27°C Braemar, Aberdeenshire 10 January 1982**

Edinburgh

Dublin

Birmingham

London

Scale
0          200 km

**Average daily temperature: 8°C**

Plymouth

## Summer temperature

Average temperature for July

Over 16°C
14–16°C
12–14°C
10–12°C
Under 10°C

**Average daily temperature: 12°C**

Edinburgh

Dublin

Birmingham

Scale
0          200 km

**Average daily temperature: 17°C**

Plymouth

**Highest-ever recorded temperature: 38°C Faversham, Kent 10 August 2003**

# Water

## Rainfall areas in the UK and Ireland

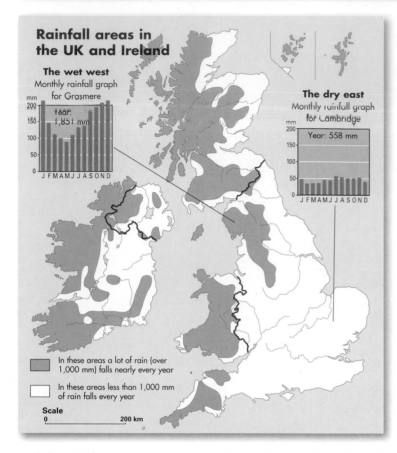

### The wet west
Monthly rainfall graph for Grasmere

Year: 1,851 mm

mm
200
150
100
50
0
J F M A M J J A S O N D

### The dry east
Monthly rainfall graph for Cambridge

Year: 558 mm

mm
200
150
100
50
0
J F M A M J J A S O N D

In these areas a lot of rain (over 1,000 mm) falls nearly every year

In these areas less than 1,000 mm of rain falls every year

Scale
0          200 km

## Reservoirs and boreholes

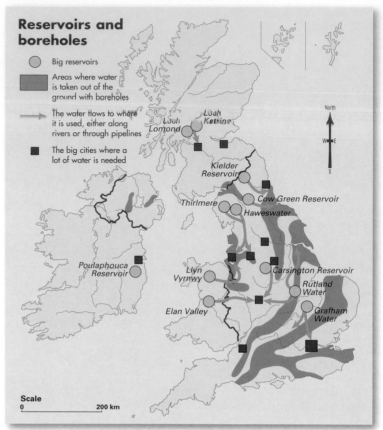

Big reservoirs

Areas where water is taken out of the ground with boreholes

The water flows to where it is used, either along rivers or through pipelines

The big cities where a lot of water is needed

North
W E
S

Loch Lomond
Loch Katrine
Kielder Reservoir
Cow Green Reservoir
Thirlmere
Haweswater
Poulaphouca Reservoir
Llyn Vyrnwy
Carsington Reservoir
Rutland Water
Elan Valley
Grafham Water

Scale
0          200 km

## Sources of river pollution

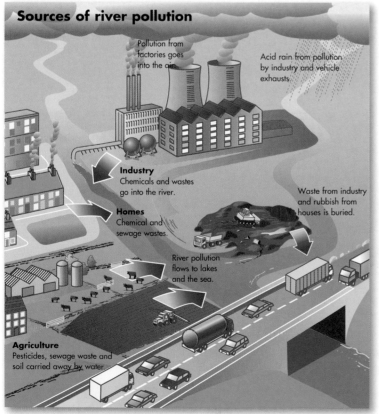

Pollution from factories goes into the air.

Acid rain from pollution by industry and vehicle exhausts.

**Industry**
Chemicals and wastes go into the river.

**Homes**
Chemical and sewage wastes.

Waste from industry and rubbish from houses is buried.

River pollution flows to lakes and the sea.

**Agriculture**
Pesticides, sewage waste and soil carried away by water

## Pollution

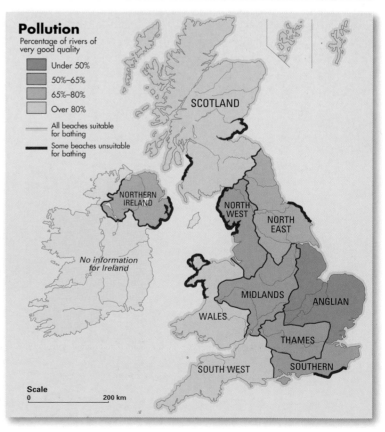

Percentage of rivers of very good quality

Under 50%

50%–65%

65%–80%

Over 80%

All beaches suitable for bathing

Some beaches unsuitable for bathing

SCOTLAND

NORTHERN IRELAND

NORTH WEST

NORTH EAST

No information for Ireland

MIDLANDS

ANGLIAN

WALES

THAMES

SOUTH WEST

SOUTHERN

Scale
0          200 km

Up to 17,400 million litres of water are used each day in the UK. Over half the water is used by people in their homes. About a third is used to make electricity. The rest is used in farms, fish farms and factories. In the UK each person uses about 150 litres of water per day. On the right are some of the ways that water is used in the home.

To make one car can use up to 40,000 litres of water. To brew one pint of beer needs 8 pints of water.

## How we use water in the home

| | |
|---|---|
| Showering and bathing | 33% |
| Flushing the toilet | 30% |
| Clothes washing | 13% |
| Washing up | 8% |
| Outdoors | 7% |
| Drinking | 4% |

## The water cycle

Condensation
Precipitation
Moist air mass moves to land
Transpiration from vegetation
Evaporation from ponds and lakes
Evaporation from soil
Evaporation from rivers
Evaporation from oceans
Ground water moves to rivers, lakes and oceans
Run off
Ocean

## Domestic water and sewage (the man-made water cycle)

Rainfall
Evaporation from the sea
Reservoirs and boreholes collect water from the ground and rivers
Clean water is put back into rivers and the sea
Water is cleaned at a treatment plant before being piped to houses, factories, schools and hospitals
Waste water is piped to sewage works for treatment

## Flooding

Around 5 million people, in 2 million properties, live in flood risk areas in England and Wales. In summer 2007 there were several periods of extreme rainfall which led to widespread flooding.

The Environment Agency has an important role in warning people about the risk of flooding, and in reducing the likelihood of flooding from rivers and the sea.

### Flood risk in England and Wales

Areas at greatest risk from flooding

Counties worst affected by flooding in summer 2007

# Farming and fishing

## Types of farm in the UK and Ireland

Dairy farms
Cows for milk, butter and cheese

Beef farms
Cows and calves for beef and veal

Sheep farms
Sheep and lambs for wool and meat

Grain and root farms
Wheat, potatoes, sugar beet and oilseed rape

Mixed farms
Livestock and grain or roots

Market gardening
Vegetables, fruit and flowers

Forests

Big cities

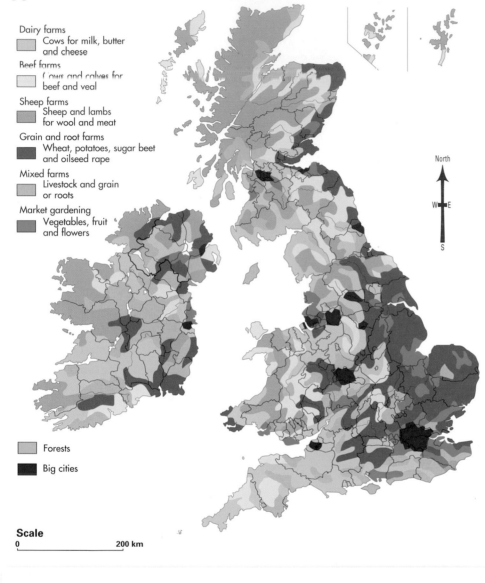

North

W E

S

Scale

0                    200 km

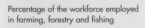

## Employment in agriculture

Percentage of the workforce employed in farming, forestry and fishing

Over 10%

2–10%

Under 10%

## How much of our food is grown in the UK?

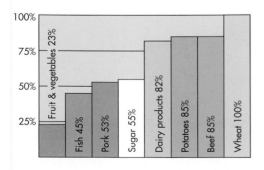

100%
75%
50%
25%

Fruit & vegetables 23%
Fish 45%
Pork 53%
Sugar 55%
Dairy products 82%
Potatoes 85%
Beef 85%
Wheat 100%

## Where does the food eaten in the UK come from?

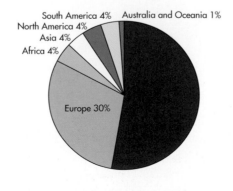

South America 4%      Australia and Oceania 1%
North America 4%
Asia 4%
Africa 4%

Europe 30%

## Fishing

Large fishing ports (over 20,000 tonnes of fish caught each year)

Other important fishing ports

Scrabster
Kinlochbervie
Ullapool
Fraserburgh
Lerwick
Peterhead
Mallaig
ATLANTIC OCEAN
NORTH SEA
Killybegs
Kirkcudbright
North Shields
Portavogie
Douglas
Kilkeel
Ardglass
Rossaveel
Howth
IRISH SEA
Milford Haven
Dunmore East
Castletown Bearhaven
CELTIC SEA
Plymouth
Brixham
Shoreham
Newlyn
ENGLISH CHANNEL

# Conservation

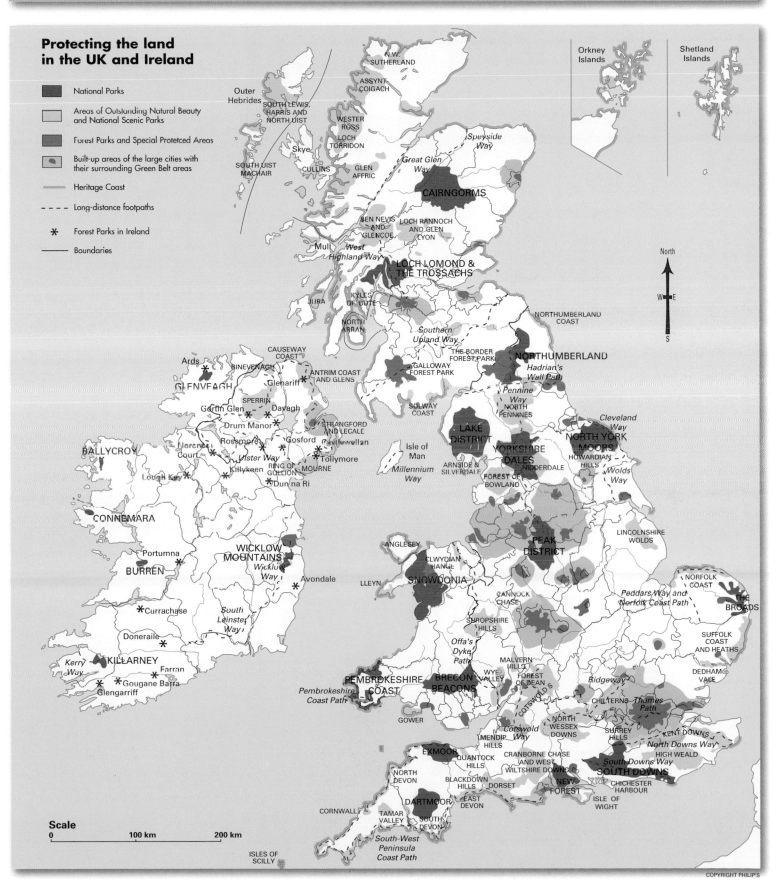

## Protecting the land in the UK and Ireland

- National Parks
- Areas of Outstanding Natural Beauty and National Scenic Parks
- Forest Parks and Special Protected Areas
- Built-up areas of the large cities with their surrounding Green Belt areas
- Heritage Coast
- - - - Long-distance footpaths
- \* Forest Parks in Ireland
- Boundaries

Orkney Islands

Shetland Islands

N.W. SUTHERLAND

ASSYNT COIGACH

Outer Hebrides

SOUTH LEWIS, HARRIS AND NORTH UIST

WESTER ROSS

Speyside Way

Skye

LOCH TORRIDON

SOUTH UIST MACHAIR

CULLINS

GLEN AFFRIC

Great Glen Way

CAIRNGORMS

BEN NEVIS AND GLENCOE

LOCH RANNOCH AND GLEN LYON

Mull

West Highland Way

LOCH LOMOND & THE TROSSACHS

JURA

KYLES OF BUTE

NORTH ARRAN

North

Southern Upland Way

NORTHUMBERLAND COAST

CAUSEWAY COAST

Ards \*

BINEVENAGH

Glenariff

ANTRIM COAST AND GLENS

THE BORDER FOREST PARK

NORTHUMBERLAND

Hadrian's Wall Path

GLENVEAGH

SPERRIN

Davagh \*

GALLOWAY FOREST PARK

Pennine Way NORTH PENNINES

Cleveland Way

Gortin Glen \*

\* \*

Drum Manor \*

SOLWAY COAST

Rossmore \*

Gosford

STRANGFORD AND LECALE

Castlewellan

LAKE DISTRICT

NORTH YORK MOORS

BALLYCROY

Florence Court

Ulster Way

RING OF GULLION

MOURNE

Isle of Man

ARNSIDE & SILVERDALE

YORKSHIRE DALES

HOVARDIAN HILLS

Killykeen \*

\* Tollymore

Millennium Way

NIDDERDALE

Wolds Way

Lough Key \*

\* Dun na Ri

FOREST OF BOWLAND

LINCOLNSHIRE WOLDS

CONNEMARA

PEAK DISTRICT

Portumna

WICKLOW MOUNTAINS

ANGLESEY

CLWYDIAN RANGE

BURREN

Wicklow Way

\* Avondale

LLEYN

SNOWDONIA

CANNOCK CHASE

NORFOLK COAST

Peddars Way and Norfolk Coast Path

THE BROADS

\* Currachase

South Leinster Way

SHROPSHIRE HILLS

SUFFOLK COAST AND HEATHS

Doneraile

Offa's Dyke Path

MALVERN HILLS

WYE VALLEY

FOREST OF DEAN

Ridgeway

CHILTERNS

Thames Path

DEDHAM VALE

Kerry Way

KILLARNEY

Farran

PEMBROKESHIRE COAST

BRECON BEACONS

COTSWOLDS

NORTH WESSEX DOWNS

SURREY HILLS

KENT DOWNS

\* Gougane Barra

Glengarriff

Pembrokeshire Coast Path

GOWER

Cotswold Way

MENDIP HILLS

CRANBORNE CHASE AND WEST WILTSHIRE DOWNS

North Downs Way

HIGH WEALD

EXMOOR

QUANTOCK HILLS

SOUTH DOWNS

South Downs Way

NORTH DEVON

BLACKDOWN HILLS

DORSET

EAST DEVON

NEW FOREST

CHICHESTER HARBOUR

ISLE OF WIGHT

CORNWALL

TAMAR VALLEY

DARTMOOR

SOUTH DEVON

South-West Peninsula Coast Path

ISLES OF SCILLY

### Scale

| 0 | 100 km | 200 km |

# Work, industry and energy

## Total workforce in the UK and Ireland

The number of people working

- Over 4 million
- 3–4 million
- 2–3 million
- Under 2 million

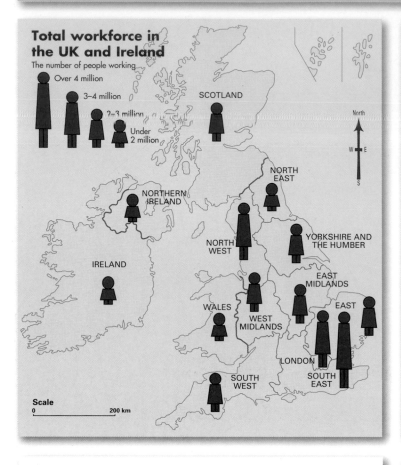

SCOTLAND

NORTHERN IRELAND

IRELAND

NORTH EAST

NORTH WEST

YORKSHIRE AND THE HUMBER

EAST MIDLANDS

WALES

WEST MIDLANDS

EAST

LONDON

SOUTH EAST

SOUTH WEST

North

Scale
0        200 km

## Employment in service industries in the UK and Ireland

- Over 90%
- 80%–90%
- Under 80%

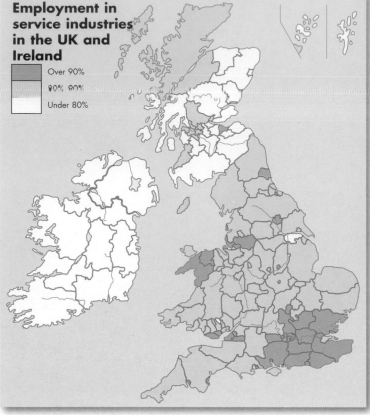

*Manufacturing industries are industries which make things. Some examples of manufactured goods are cars, steel, textiles and clothes.*

*Service industries do not make things. They provide a service to people. Shops, hotels and banks are examples of service industries.*

## Unemployment

Percentage of the workforce unemployed

- Under 8%
- 8–10%
- Over 10%

## Employment in manufacturing

Percentage of the workforce employed in manufacturing

- Under 10%
- 10–15%
- Over 15%

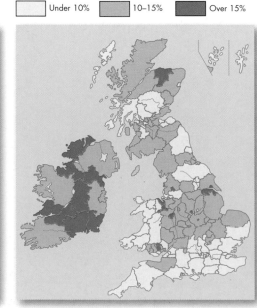

## Income

The average amount each person earns each week

- Under £450
- £450–£500
- Over £500

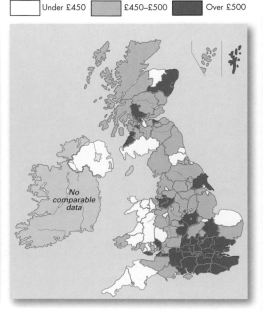

No comparable data

## Sources of energy used in the UK

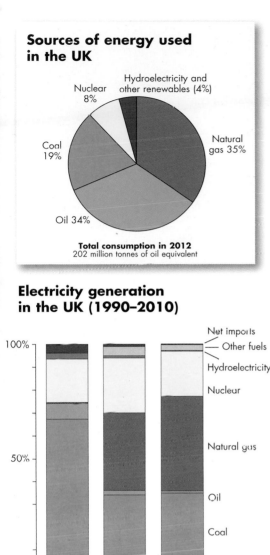

Nuclear 8%

Hydroelectricity and other renewables (4%)

Coal 19%

Natural gas 35%

Oil 34%

**Total consumption in 2012**
202 million tonnes of oil equivalent

## Electricity generation in the UK (1990–2010)

Net imports
Other fuels
Hydroelectricity
Nuclear
Natural gas
Oil
Coal

100%

50%

0%

1990    2000    2010

This bar-chart shows the different types of fuel that are used to make electricity in the UK. The use of coal and oil in the generation of electricity has dropped between 1990 and 2010. However, the use of natural gas has greatly increased.

## Renewable energy in the UK

Renewable sources used to generate electricity (in million tonnes of oil equivalent)

|                   | 2002 | 2006 | 2009 | 2012 |
|-------------------|------|------|------|------|
| Biofuels          | 1.3  | 2.1  | 1.8  | 3.2  |
| Hydroelectricity  | 1.1  | 1.0  | 1.2  | 1.2  |
| Wind power        | 0.1  | 0.1  | 0.1  | 0.2  |
| Solar             | 0    | 0    | 0    | 0.1  |
| Other             | 0    | 0.8  | 2.6  | 6.0  |
| Total renewables  | 2.5  | 4.0  | 5.7  | 10.7 |

In 2012 5.3% of electricity in the UK was generated by renewable energy sources. This is short of the government's target to increase this to 20% by 2020.

# Energy sources in the UK and Ireland

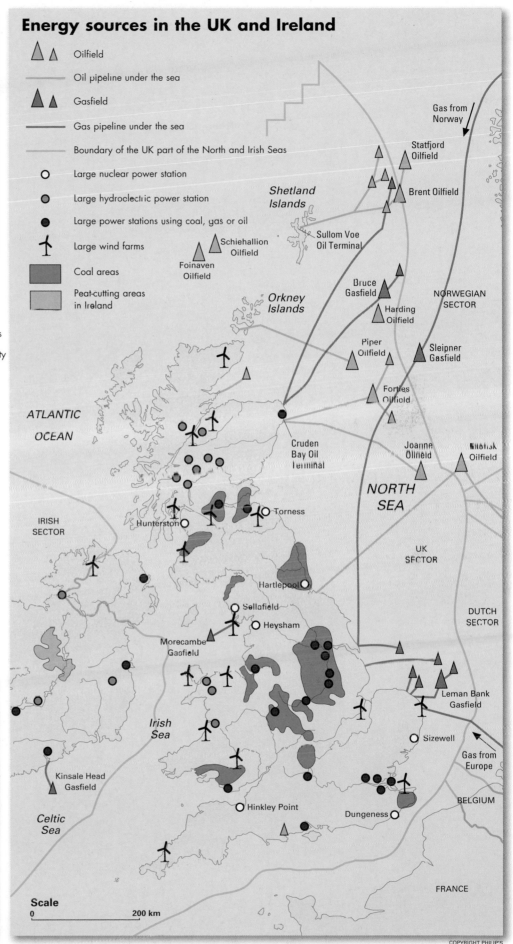

Oilfield

Oil pipeline under the sea

Gasfield

Gas pipeline under the sea

Boundary of the UK part of the North and Irish Seas

○ Large nuclear power station

◔ Large hydroelectric power station

● Large power stations using coal, gas or oil

✈ Large wind farms

Coal areas

Peat-cutting areas in Ireland

Gas from Norway

Statfjord Oilfield

Shetland Islands

Brent Oilfield

Sullom Voe Oil Terminal

Schiehallion Oilfield

Foinaven Oilfield

Bruce Gasfield

NORWEGIAN SECTOR

Harding Oilfield

Orkney Islands

Piper Oilfield

Sleipner Gasfield

ATLANTIC OCEAN

Forties Oilfield

Cruden Bay Oil Terminal

Joanne Oilfield

Ellon Oilfield

NORTH SEA

IRISH SECTOR

Torness

Hunterston

UK SECTOR

Hartlepool

Sellafield

DUTCH SECTOR

Heysham

Morecambe Gasfield

Leman Bank Gasfield

Irish Sea

Sizewell

Kinsale Head Gasfield

Gas from Europe

BELGIUM

Celtic Sea

Hinkley Point

Dungeness

FRANCE

**Scale**
0        200 km

# Transport

There are about 407 thousand kilometres of road in the UK. The total number of cars, buses, lorries and motorbikes is 35 million. That is more than half the number of people in the UK. The maps on this page show the motorways and some main roads in the UK and the number of cars in the different regions. At the bottom of the page there are tables showing the road distances between important towns.

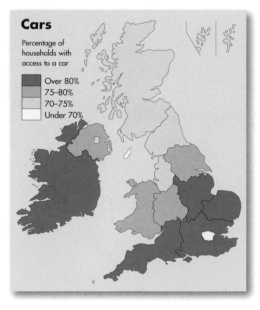

## Cars

Percentage of households with access to a car

- Over 80%
- 75–80%
- 70–75%
- Under 70%

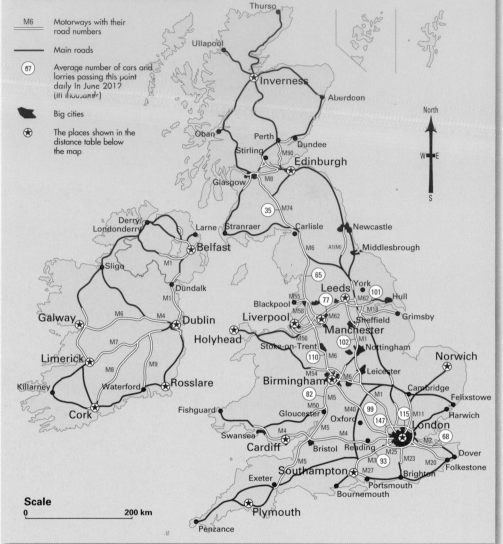

### Roads in the UK and Ireland

- **M6** — Motorways with their road numbers
- —— Main roads
- (87) — Average number of cars and lorries passing this point daily in June 2012 (in thousands)
- ◣ Big cities
- ✪ The places shown in the distance table below the map

**Scale**

0 — 200 km

| UK | Birmingham | Cardiff | Edinburgh | Holyhead | Inverness | Leeds | Liverpool | London | Manchester | Norwich | Plymouth | Southampton |
|---|---|---|---|---|---|---|---|---|---|---|---|---|
| Birmingham | | 163 | 460 | 246 | 716 | 179 | 151 | 179 | 130 | 249 | 320 | 206 |
| Cardiff | 163 | | 587 | 341 | 843 | 341 | 264 | 249 | 277 | 381 | 259 | 192 |
| Edinburgh | 460 | 587 | | 489 | 256 | 320 | 338 | 608 | 336 | 586 | 790 | 669 |
| Holyhead | 246 | 341 | 489 | | 745 | 262 | 151 | 420 | 198 | 481 | 528 | 455 |
| Inverness | 716 | 843 | 256 | 745 | | 579 | 605 | 864 | 604 | 842 | 1049 | 925 |
| Leeds | 179 | 341 | 320 | 262 | 579 | | 119 | 306 | 64 | 277 | 502 | 378 |
| Liverpool | 151 | 264 | 338 | 151 | 605 | 119 | | 330 | 55 | 360 | 452 | 357 |
| London | 179 | 249 | 608 | 420 | 864 | 306 | 330 | | 309 | 172 | 343 | 127 |
| Manchester | 130 | 277 | 336 | 198 | 604 | 64 | 55 | 309 | | 306 | 457 | 325 |
| Norwich | 249 | 381 | 586 | 481 | 842 | 277 | 360 | 172 | 306 | | 515 | 299 |
| Plymouth | 320 | 259 | 790 | 528 | 1049 | 502 | 452 | 343 | 457 | 515 | | 246 |
| Southampton | 206 | 192 | 669 | 455 | 925 | 378 | 357 | 127 | 325 | 299 | 246 | |

### Road distances

The distance tables are in kilometres, but distances on road signposts in the UK are in miles.
A mile is longer than a kilometre.
1 mile = 1.6 kilometres. 1 kilometre = 0.6 mile.

| Ireland | Belfast | Cork | Dublin | Galway | Limerick | Rosslare |
|---|---|---|---|---|---|---|
| Belfast | | 418 | 160 | 300 | 222 | 306 |
| Cork | 418 | | 257 | 193 | 97 | 190 |
| Dublin | 160 | 257 | | 210 | 193 | 137 |
| Galway | 300 | 193 | 210 | | 97 | 249 |
| Limerick | 222 | 97 | 193 | 97 | | 193 |
| Rosslare | 306 | 190 | 137 | 249 | 193 | |

## Railways

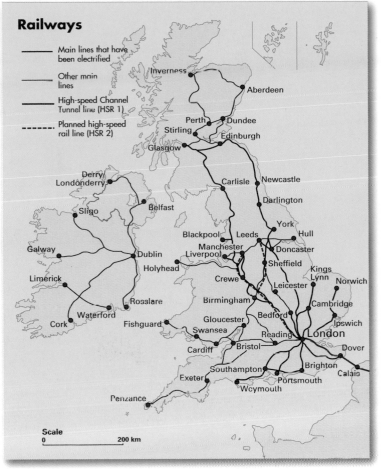

- ▬▬ Main lines that have been electrified
- ▬▬ Other main lines
- ▬▬ High-speed Channel Tunnel line (HSR 1)
- ▪▪▪▪ Planned high-speed rail line (HSR 2)

Inverness
Aberdeen
Perth · Dundee
Stirling
Edinburgh
Glasgow
Derry/Londonderry
Carlisle · Newcastle
Darlington
Belfast
Sligo
York · Hull
Galway
Blackpool · Leeds
Dublin
Manchester · Doncaster
Limerick
Liverpool
Sheffield
Holyhead
Crewe
Kings Lynn
Leicester · Norwich
Rosslare
Birmingham · Cambridge
Waterford
Bedford · Ipswich
Cork
Fishguard
Gloucester
Swansea · Reading · London
Cardiff · Bristol · Dover
Southampton · Brighton
Exeter · Portsmouth · Calais
Weymouth
Penzance

Scale
0 ——— 200 km

## Manchester – the daily flow of cars

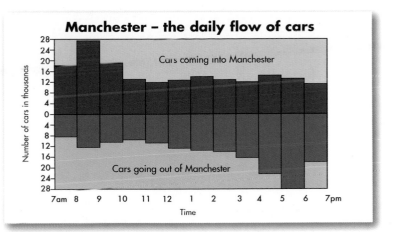

Number of cars in thousands

Cars coming into Manchester

Cars going out of Manchester

7am 8 9 10 11 12 1 2 3 4 5 6 7pm
Time

## High-speed rail

High-speed rail lines in Europe are shown in red on the map. Trains can travel at over 200 km/h on these lines.

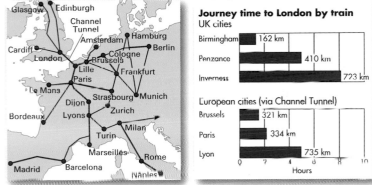

Glasgow · Edinburgh
Channel Tunnel
Cardiff · London
Amsterdam · Hamburg · Berlin
Cologne
Brussels
Lille · Frankfurt
Paris
Le Mans · Strasbourg · Munich
Dijon · Zurich
Bordeaux · Lyons
Turin · Milan
Marseilles · Rome
Madrid · Barcelona · Naples

### Journey time to London by train

**UK cities**

| | |
|---|---|
| Birmingham | 162 km |
| Penzance | 410 km |
| Inverness | 723 km |

**European cities (via Channel Tunnel)**

| | |
|---|---|
| Brussels | 321 km |
| Paris | 334 km |
| Lyon | 735 km |

0 2 4 6 8 10
Hours

## Ports and ferries

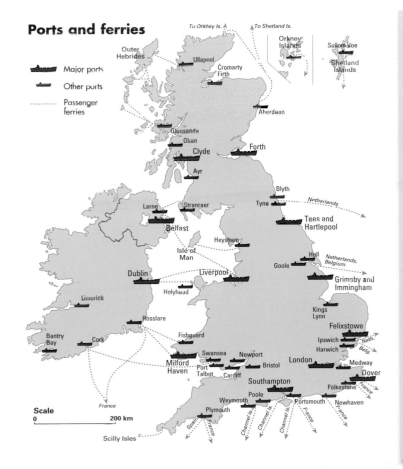

- 🚢 Major ports
- ⛴ Other ports
- ⋯⋯ Passenger ferries

To Orkney Is.
To Shetland Is.
Orkney Islands
Outer Hebrides
Sullom Voe
Shetland Islands
Ullapool
Cromarty Firth
Aberdeen
Glensanda
Oban
Forth
Clyde
Ayr
Blyth
Larne · Stranraer
Tyne · Netherlands
Belfast
Tees and Hartlepool
Heysham
Isle of Man
Hull · Netherlands, Belgium
Dublin
Liverpool
Goole
Holyhead
Grimsby and Immingham
Limerick
Kings Lynn
Rosslare
Felixstowe
Bantry Bay
Ipswich · Neth.
Cork
Harwich
Fishguard · Belg.
Swansea · Newport
Milford Haven
Bristol · London · Medway
Port Talbot · Cardiff
Southampton · Dover · France
Weymouth · Poole · Folkestone
Plymouth · Portsmouth · Newhaven · France
Spain France · Channel Is. · France
Scilly Isles

Scale
0 ——— 200 km

## Airports

- ✈ Over half the people are travelling within the UK or Ireland (Domestic airports)
- ✈ Over half the people are travelling to other countries (International airports)

Inverness · Aberdeen
Glasgow International
Edinburgh
Glasgow Prestwick
Belfast International
Newcastle
George Best Belfast City
Isle of Man
Leeds Bradford International
Dublin
Liverpool John Lennon
Doncaster/Sheffield
Manchester
Shannon
East Midlands International
Birmingham
London Luton
London Stansted
Cork
Bristol
Cardiff
London City
London Heathrow
London Gatwick
Exeter International
Bournemouth
Southampton

Scale
0 ——— 200 km

## Country names

The map on the left shows the **British Isles**, which is made up of the two large islands of **Great Britain** and **Ireland** and many smaller islands. The islands contain two countries, the **United Kingdom** and **Ireland**. The full name of the United Kingdom is The United Kingdom of Great Britain and Northern Ireland. It has four parts: **England**, **Wales**, **Scotland** and **Northern Ireland**. It is known for short as the United Kingdom, UK or Britain. The whole country is often wrongly called England. Ireland is sometimes shown as Eire (on its stamps), which is the name of Ireland in the Irish language.

● Capital cities

## Countries and regions

The map shows the Standard Regions of the United Kingdom. The boundaries follow those of the counties shown on page 19. Large bodies like the Health Service and Water and Power providers divide the country up into their own regions. Ireland is divided into four historic provinces.

## Counties and unitary authorities

England and Wales are divided into counties, unitary authorities and boroughs.

Scotland is divided into regions and unitary authorities, and Northern Ireland into districts.

Ireland is divided into counties.

| Area data | |
|---|---|
| | Area in square kilometres |
| England | 130,439 |
| Wales | 20,768 |
| Scotland | 77,167 |
| Northern Ireland | 13,483 |
| **United Kingdom** | **241,857** |
| **Isle of Man** | **572** |
| **Channel Islands** | **195** |
| **Ireland** | **68,896** |

# Counties and Unitary Authorities of the UK and Ireland

Authorities which are too small to name on the map are numbered and listed separately.

## SCOTLAND
1. ABERDEEN CITY
2. DUNDEE CITY
3. WEST DUNBARTONSHIRE
4. EAST DUNBARTONSHIRE
5. CITY OF GLASGOW
6. INVERCLYDE
7. RENFREWSHIRE
8. EAST RENFREWSHIRE
9. NORTH LANARKSHIRE
10. FALKIRK
11. CLACKMANNANSHIRE
12. WEST LOTHIAN
13. CITY OF EDINBURGH
14. MIDLOTHIAN

## WALES
15. SWANSEA
16. NEATH PORT TALBOT
17. BRIDGEND
18. RHONDDA CYNON TAFF
19. MERTHYR TYDFIL
20. CAERPHILLY
21. BLAENAU GWENT
22. TORFAEN
23. CARDIFF
24. NEWPORT

The Channel Islands and the Isle of Man are dependencies of the Crown and have their own parliaments. They are not part of the United Kingdom.

## ENGLAND
25. HARTLEPOOL
26. DARLINGTON
27. STOCKTON-ON-TEES
28. MIDDLESBROUGH
29. REDCAR AND CLEVELAND
30. BLACKPOOL
31. BLACKBURN WITH DARWEN
32. HALTON
33. WARRINGTON
34. KINGSTON UPON HULL
35. NORTH EAST LINCOLNSHIRE
36. STOKE-ON-TRENT
37. TELFORD AND WREKIN
38. DERBY CITY
39. CITY OF NOTTINGHAM
40. LEICESTER CITY
41. RUTLAND
42. PETERBOROUGH
43. MILTON KEYNES
44. LUTON
45. NORTH SOMERSET
46. CITY OF BRISTOL
47. BATH AND N. E. SOMERSET
48. SWINDON
49. READING
50. WOKINGHAM
51. WINDSOR AND MAIDENHEAD
52. SLOUGH
53. BRACKNELL FOREST
54. THURROCK
55. SOUTHEND-ON-SEA
56. MEDWAY
57. PLYMOUTH
58. TORBAY
59. POOLE
60. BOURNEMOUTH
61. SOUTHAMPTON
62. PORTSMOUTH
63. BRIGHTON AND HOVE
64. CHESHIRE WEST AND CHESTER
65. CHESHIRE EAST
66. BEDFORD
67. CENTRAL BEDFORDSHIRE

Capital cities

Scale
0    100 km    200 km

19

# People, cities and towns

## Old people and young people

 In these counties, young people are a large group in the population (over 20%). On this map young people are those aged under 15 years old.

In these counties, old people are a large group in the population (over 20%). On this map old people are those aged over 65 years old.

Look at the colours on the map above. Can you think of some reasons why some counties have more older people than others?

## People in the UK and Ireland

Number of people per square kilometre in 2011

- Over 500 – very high density
- 100–500 – high density
- 50–100 – medium density
- Under 50 – low density

*The average density for the UK is 261 people per square km.*

*The average density for Ireland is 67 people per square km.*

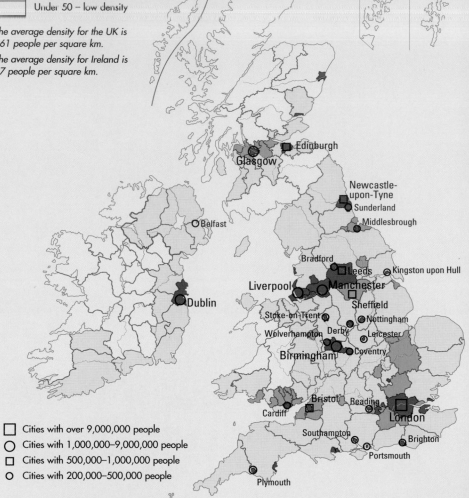

- ☐ Cities with over 9,000,000 people
- ◯ Cities with 1,000,000–9,000,000 people
- ▢ Cities with 500,000–1,000,000 people
- ○ Cities with 200,000–500,000 people

## Country population data

|  | 1901 | 1951 | 2012 |
|---|---|---|---|
|  |  | millions |  |
| England | 30.5 | 41.2 | 52.9 |
| Wales | 2.0 | 2.6 | 3.1 |
| Scotland | 4.5 | 5.1 | 5.3 |
| Northern Ireland | 1.2 | 1.4 | 1.8 |
| **United Kingdom** | **38.2** | **50.3** | **63.1** |
| **Ireland** | **3.2** | **2.9** | **4.7** |

## Changing numbers

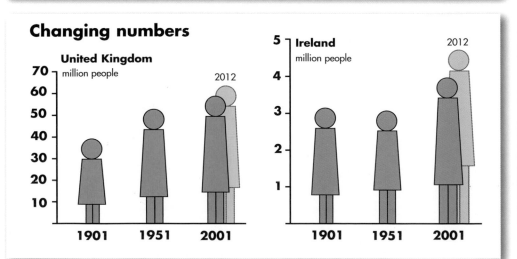

United Kingdom million people

Ireland million people

# Cities and towns of the UK and Ireland

**Map scale**  This distance is 400 kilometres

0 ————————————— 400 km

**Map information**

**Height of land**

| | metres |
|---|---|
| | Over 1,000 |
| | 500–1,000 |
| | 200–500 |
| | 0–200 |
| | Below sea level |
| | Sea |

**Cities and towns**

**London** ■ Over 9,000,000 people
**Dublin** ■ 1,000,000 – 9,000,000 people
**Leeds** ● 500,000 – 1,000,000 people
**Plymouth** ● 200,000 – 500,000 people
Oxford ● 100,000 – 200,000 people
Guildford ● 50,000 – 100,000 people
*Dover* • Under 50,000 people

North

ATLANTIC OCEAN

North Sea

Irish Sea

Celtic Sea

SCOTLAND

NORTHERN IRELAND

IRELAND

UNITED KINGDOM

ENGLAND

WALES

FRANCE

Shetland Islands

Orkney Islands

Outer Hebrides

Inner Hebrides

Lerwick
Kirkwall
Thurso
Wick
Stornoway
Helmsdale
Lairg
Golspie
Ullapool
Invergordon
Dingwall
Nairn
Elgin
Banff
Fraserburgh
Peterhead
Inverness
Huntly
Inverurie
Portree
Aviemore
Aberdeen
Mallaig
Ballater
Stonehaven
Tobermory
Fort William
Forfar
Montrose
Arbroath
Oban
Perth
Dundee
St. Andrews
Stirling
Glenrothes
Kirkcaldy
Dunbar
Dumbarton
Dunfermline
Greenock
Glasgow
Edinburgh
Paisley
Hamilton
Berwick-upon-Tweed
East Kilbride
Irvine
Kilmarnock
Galashiels
Jedburgh
Ayr
Hawick
Alnwick
Campbeltown
Girvan
Dumfries
Newcastle-upon-Tyne
South Shields
Sunderland
Gateshead
Durham
Hartlepool
Carlisle
Darlington
Redcar
Middlesbrough
Workington
Stockton
Whitehaven
Scarborough
Barrow-in-Furness
Bridlington
Douglas
Isle of Man
Lancaster
Harrogate
York
Kingston upon Hull
Buncrana
Coleraine
Letterkenny
Derry/Londonderry
Ballymena
Larne
Donegal
Antrim
Bangor
Omagh
Belfast
Bundoran
Portadown
Lisburn
Lurgan
Enniskillen
Armagh
Ballina
Sligo
Newry
Castlebar
Cavan
Dundalk
Westport
Roscommon
Longford
Drogheda
Athlone
Mullingar
Blackpool
Burnley
Keighley
Leeds
Bradford
Galway
Ballinasloe
Tullamore
Preston
Blackburn
Halifax
Huddersfield
Scunthorpe
Grimsby
Bolton
Barnsley
Doncaster
Dublin
Holyhead
Manchester
Oldham
Rotherham
Sheffield
Lincoln
Liverpool
Stockport
Louth
Dun Laoghaire
Warrington
Chesterfield
Skegness
Bray
Bangor
Chester
Crewe
Mansfield
Boston
Ennis
Wrexham
Derby
Nottingham
Cromer
Limerick
Nenagh
Carlow
Stoke-on-Trent
Stafford
Grantham
King's Lynn
Great Yarmouth
Kilrush
Thurles
Kilkenny
Arklow
Shrewsbury
Telford
Norwich
Tipperary
Pwllheli
Nuneaton
Leicester
Peterborough
Lowestoft
Clonmel
Carrick-on-Suir
Welshpool
Wolverhampton
Corby
Thetford
Tralee
Wexford
Aberystwyth
Birmingham
Coventry
Rugby
Cambridge
Bury St. Edmunds
Ipswich
Dingle
Mallow
Waterford
Rosslare Harbour
Worcester
Northampton
Bedford
Ely
Killarney
Youghal
Dungarvan
Hereford
Milton Keynes
Stevenage
Harwich
Felixstowe
Cork
Bandon
Cóbh
Fishguard
Carmarthen
Brecon
Cheltenham
Oxford
Luton
Harlow
Chelmsford
Colchester
Bantry
Haverfordwest
Merthyr Tydfil
Gloucester
High Wycombe
Watford
Basildon
Milford Haven
Neath
Cwmbran
Swindon
Slough
Southend
Pembroke
Llanelli
Rhondda
Newport
Bristol
Newbury
Reading
London
Margate
Swansea
Port Talbot
Cardiff
Bath
Basingstoke
Guildford
Reigate
Chatham
Canterbury
Barry
Maidstone
Dover
Weston-super-Mare
Salisbury
Winchester
Crawley
Ashford
Folkestone
Barnstaple
Taunton
Southampton
Havant
Hastings
Calais
Bude
Yeovil
Bournemouth
Poole
Portsmouth
Brighton
Eastbourne
Boulogne-sur-Mer
Newquay
Exeter
Newport
Worthing
Exmouth
Weymouth
Truro
Torquay
St. Austell
Plymouth
Falmouth
Penzance

West from Greenwich   East from Greenwich

COPYRIGHT PHILIP'S

21

# Tourism

## Tourism in the UK and Ireland

● Main holiday destinations
● Other major tourist attractions

North
W—E
S

Scale
0 — 200 km

Inverness, Nairn, Loch Ness, Aviemore, Fort William, Montrose, Oban, Arbroath, Dunoon, Glasgow, Dunbar, Edinburgh, Giant's Causeway, Ayr, Portrush, Hadrian's Wall, Bangor, Bundoran, Windermere, Fountains Abbey, Whitby, Sligo, Scarborough, Lough Key Nature Park, Morecambe, Flamingo Land, Killykeen Forest Park, Douglas, Bridlington, Knock Shrine, Blackpool, York, Xscape, Tayto Park, Southport, Saltaire, Galway, DUBLIN, Llandudno, Manchester, Liverpool, Cliffs of Moher, Powerscourt Castle, Bray, Derwent Valley Mills, Skegness, Kilkee, Gwynedd Castles, Chester, Alton Towers, Limerick, Arklow, Great Yarmouth, Bunratty Castle, Ironbridge Gorge, Blarney Castle, Aberystwyth, Drayton Manor, Thetford Forest Park, Killarney, Stratford-upon-Avon, Cork, Fota Wildlife Park, Tenby, Blaenavon, Blenheim, Lee Valley Regional Park, Clacton, LONDON, Southend, Legoland Windsor, Greenwich, Weston-super-Mare, Bath, Thorpe Park, Chessington, Margate, Minehead, Stonehenge, Brighton, Canterbury, Worthing, Hastings, Eastbourne, Newquay, Bournemouth, St. Ives, Eden Project, Torbay, Weymouth

## Tourist traffic

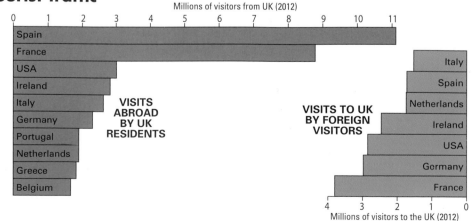

**Millions of visitors from UK (2012)**

VISITS ABROAD BY UK RESIDENTS

Spain, France, USA, Ireland, Italy, Germany, Portugal, Netherlands, Greece, Belgium

VISITS TO UK BY FOREIGN VISITORS

Italy, Spain, Netherlands, Ireland, USA, Germany, France

Millions of visitors to the UK (2012)

## UK tourist attractions
(number of visitors in millions, 2012)

| | |
|---|---|
| 1. British Museum, London | 5.6 |
| 2. Tate Modern, London | 5.3 |
| 3. National Gallery, London | 5.2 |
| 4. Natural History Museum, London | 5.0 |
| 5. Victoria and Albert Museum, London | 3.2 |
| 6. Science Museum, London | 3.0 |
| 7. Tower of London | 2.4 |
| 8. National Portrait Gallery, London | 2.1 |
| 9. National Museum of Scotland, Edinburgh | 1.9 |
| 10. St Paul's Cathedral, London | 1.8 |
| 11. Old Royal Naval College, Greenwich | 1.8 |
| 12. Westminster Abbey, London | 1.8 |
| 13. Tate Britain, London | 1.5 |
| 14. British Library, London | 1.4 |
| 15. Chester Zoo | 1.4 |
| 16. Edinburgh Castle | 1.2 |
| 17. Royal Academy of Arts, London | 1.2 |
| 18. National Maritime Museum, Greenwich | 1.1 |
| 19. Roman Baths and Pump Room, Bath | 1.1 |
| 20. Stonehenge, Wiltshire | 1.0 |

## Ireland tourist attractions
(number of visitors in millions, 2012)

| | |
|---|---|
| 1. Guinness Storehouse, Dublin | 1.1 |
| 2. Dublin Zoo | 1.0 |
| 3. Cliffs of Moher, Clare | 0.9 |
| 4. National Aquatic Centre, Dublin | 0.8 |
| 5. National Gallery, Dublin | 0.7 |
| 6. Book of Kells, Dublin | 0.6 |
| 7. National Botanic Gardens, Dublin | 0.5 |
| 8. Tayto Park, Meath | 0.4 |
| 9. St Patrick's Cathedral, Dublin | 0.4 |
| 10. Fota Wildlife Park, Cork | 0.4 |

## World tourist attractions
(number of foreign visitors in millions, 2012)

| | |
|---|---|
| 1. France | 83.0 |
| 2. USA | 67.0 |
| 3. China | 57.7 |
| 4. Spain | 57.7 |
| 5. Italy | 46.4 |
| 6. Saudi Arabia | 43.7 |
| 7. Germany | 30.4 |
| 8. UK | 29.3 |
| 9. Russia | 25.7 |
| 10. Malaysia | 25.0 |
| 11. Austria | 24.2 |
| 12. Hong Kong | 23.8 |
| 13. Mexico | 23.4 |
| 14. Ukraine | 23.0 |
| 15. Thailand | 22.4 |

# International organizations

## United Nations

The UN is the largest international organization in the world. The headquarters are in New York and 193 countries are members. It was formed in 1945 to help solve world problems and to help keep world peace. The UN sends peacekeeping forces to areas where there are problems.

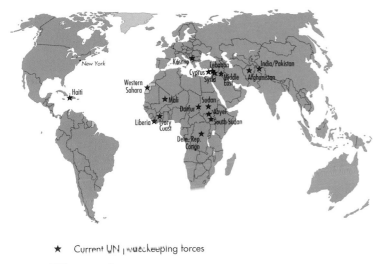

★  Current UN peacekeeping forces

   UN member countries

## European Union

| Population (million people) | |
| --- | --- |
| Austria | 8 |
| Belgium | 10 |
| Bulgaria | 7 |
| Croatia | 4 |
| Cyprus | 1 |
| Czech Republic | 10 |
| Denmark | 6 |
| Estonia | 1 |
| Finland | 5 |
| France | 66 |
| Germany | 81 |
| Greece | 11 |
| Hungary | 10 |
| Ireland | 5 |
| Italy | 61 |
| Latvia | 2 |
| Lithuania | 4 |
| Luxembourg | 0.5 |
| Malta | 0.4 |
| Netherlands | 17 |
| Poland | 38 |
| Portugal | 11 |
| Romania | 22 |
| Slovak Republic | 5 |
| Slovenia | 2 |
| Spain | 47 |
| Sweden | 9 |
| UK | 63 |

   EU member countries

*The EU was first formed in 1951. Six countries were members. Now there are 28 countries in the EU. These countries meet to discuss agriculture, industry and trade as well as social and political issues. The headquarters are in Brussels. Cyprus, the Czech Republic, Estonia, Hungary, Latvia, Lithuania, Malta, Poland, the Slovak Republic and Slovenia joined the EU in 2004. Bulgaria and Romania joined in 2007, Croatia in 2013.*

## The Commonwealth

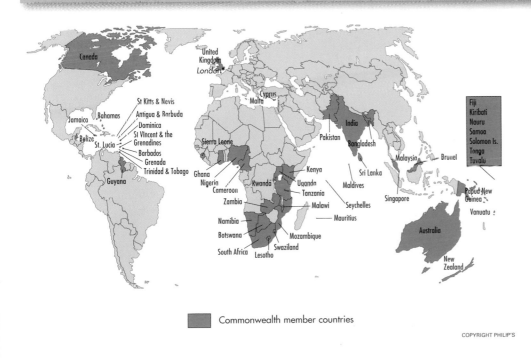

   Commonwealth member countries

The Commonwealth is a group of 53 independent countries which used to belong to the British Empire. It is organized by a group of people called the Secretariat which is based in London. Queen Elizabeth II is the head of the Commonwealth. About every two years the heads of the different governments meet to discuss world problems. These meetings are held in different countries in the Commonwealth.

23

# England and Wales

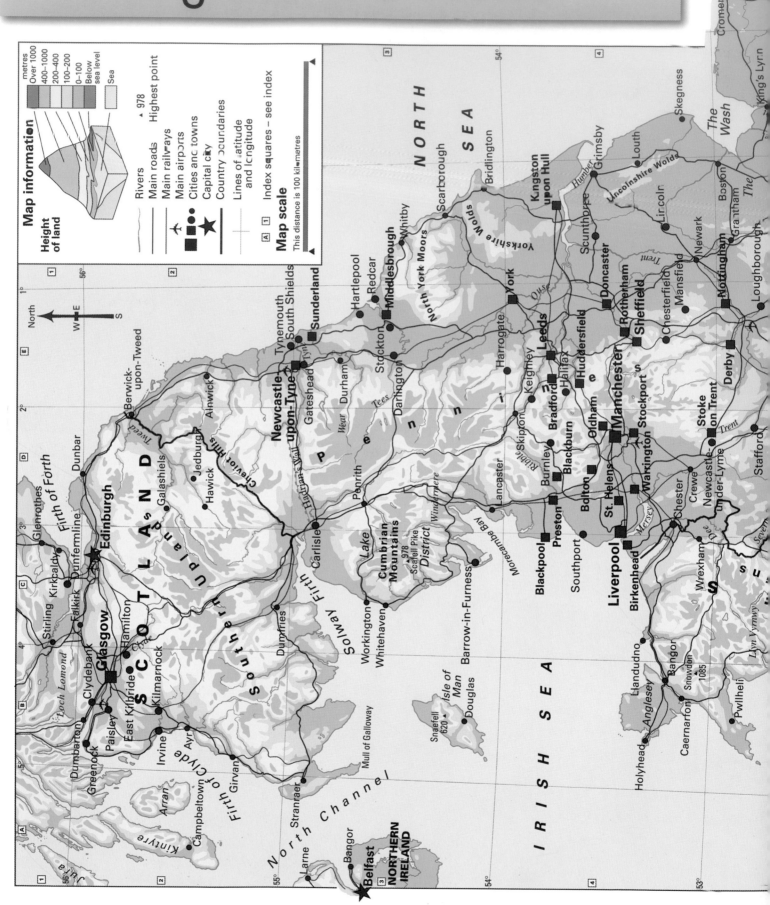

**Map information**

**Height of land**

| metres | |
|---|---|
| | Over 1000 |
| | 400–1000 |
| | 200–400 |
| | 100–200 |
| | 0–100 |
| | Below sea level |
| | Sea |

▲ 978 Highest point

Rivers
Main roads
Main railways
✈ Main airports
● Cities and towns
★ Capital city
Country boundaries
Lines of latitude and longitude

Ⓐ 1 Index squares – see index

**Map scale**

This distance is 100 kilometres

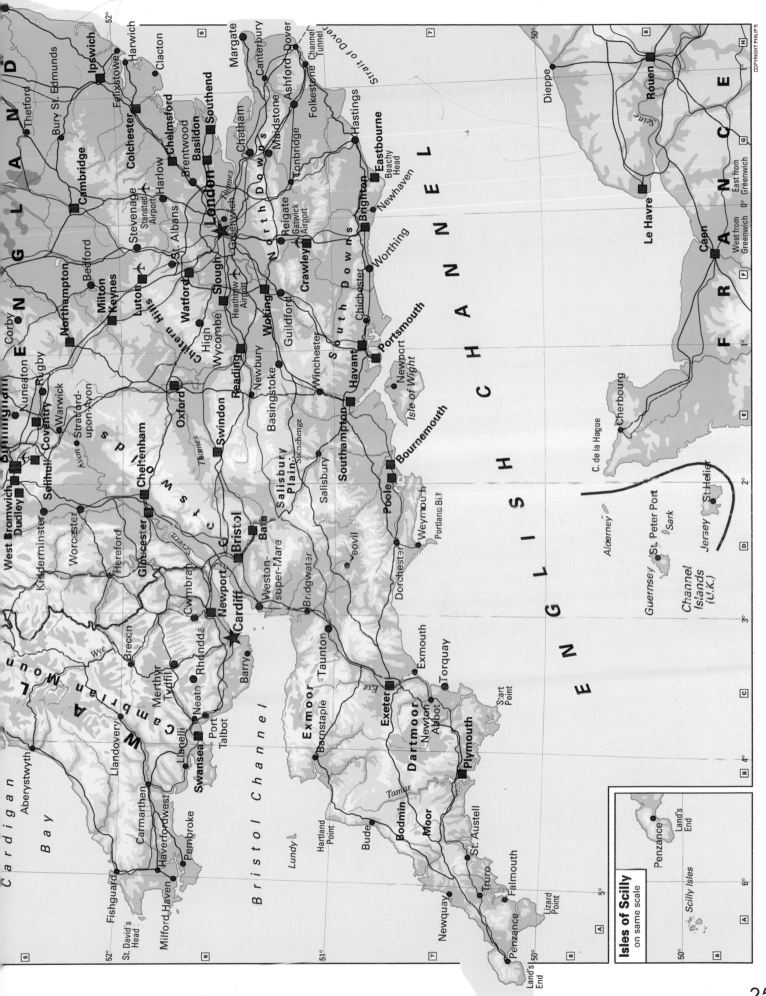

ENGLAND

FRANCE

ENGLISH CHANNEL

Bristol Channel

Cardigan Bay

WALES

North Downs

South Downs

Chiltern Hills

Salisbury Plain

Exmoor

Dartmoor

Bodmin Moor

Cambrian Mountains

Isle of Wight

Channel Islands (U.K.)

Strait of Dover

Seine

Cotswolds

Thetford · Bury St. Edmunds · Ipswich · Harwich · Felixstowe · Clacton
Cambridge · Colchester · Chelmsford · Harlow · Brentwood · Basildon · Southend · Margate · Canterbury
Bedford · Stevenage · Stansted Airport · St. Albans · Luton · Milton Keynes · Northampton
Corby · Kuneaton · Rugby · Warwick · Stratford-upon-Avon · Coventry · Solihull
Birmingham · West Bromwich · Dudley · Kidderminster · Worcester · Hereford
London · Greenwich · Slough · Watford · Heathrow Airport · Woking · Guildford · Gatwick Airport · Crawley · Reigate · Tonbridge · Maidstone · Chatham · Ashford · Dover · Folkestone · Channel Tunnel · Hastings · Eastbourne · Beachy Head · Newhaven · Brighton · Worthing · Chichester
High Wycombe · Reading · Newbury · Basingstoke · Winchester · Havant · Portsmouth · Southampton · Newport
Oxford · Swindon · Cheltenham · Gloucester · Stonehenge · Salisbury · Bournemouth · Poole · Weymouth · Portland Bill
Bristol · Bath · Weston-super-Mare · Bridgwater · Yeovil · Dorchester
Newport · Cardiff · Barry · Bridgwater · Taunton · Exmoor · Barnstaple · Exeter · Newton Abbot · Torquay · Exmouth · Start Point
Cwmbran · Rhondda · Merthyr Tydfil · Neath · Swansea · Llanelli · Port Talbot · Brecon · Llandovery · Carmarthen · Haverfordwest · Pembroke · Milford Haven · Fishguard · St. David's Head
Plymouth · Tamar · Dartmoor · Bodmin Moor · Bude · Hartland Point · St. Austell · Newquay · Truro · Falmouth · Penzance · Land's End · Lizard Point

Le Havre · Caen · Rouen · Dieppe · Cherbourg · C. de la Hague · Alderney · Guernsey · St. Peter Port · Sark · Jersey · St. Helier

West from Greenwich · East from Greenwich

Wye · Avon · Severn · Thames · Exe

Lundy

Newhaven

Lyme Bay

St. David's Head

Portland Bill

Start Point

Lizard Point

Land's End

## Isles of Scilly
on same scale

Penzance · Land's End · Scilly Isles

# Scotland and Ireland

**Orkney Islands** on same scale

Westray, Sanday, Rousay, Stronsay, Mainland, Kirkwall, Hoy, South Ronaldsay, Pentland Firth, John o' Groats

North, W–E

Cape Wrath, Thurso, John o' Groats, Wick, Helmsdale, Lairg, Golspie, Ullapool, Invergordon, Moray Firth, Elgin, Banff, Fraserburgh, Keith, Peterhead, Dingwall, Nairn, Huntly, Inverness, Spey, Inverurie, Dyce, Loch Ness, Glen Mor, Aviemore, Westhill, Aberdeen, Cairn Gorm 1245, Don, Dee, Ballater, Stonehaven, Portree, Skye, Kyle of Lochalsh, North West Highlands, Grampian Mountains, Pitlochry, Montrose, Forfar, Arbroath, Ben Nevis 1344, Fort William, Glen Coe, Tay, Dundee, St. Andrews, Crianlarich, Perth, Oban, Callander, Glenrothes, Firth of Forth, Loch Awe, Loch Lomond, Stirling, Kirkcaldy, Dunfermline, Dunbar, Dumbarton, Cumbernauld, Falkirk, Clydebank, Glasgow, Edinburgh, Greenock, Paisley, Hamilton, Berwick-upon-Tweed, Bute, East Kilbride, Clyde, Galashiels, Irvine, Troon, Kilmarnock, Tweed, Ayr, Jedburgh, Hawick, Alnwick, Campbeltown, Arran, Southern Uplands, Cheviot Hills, Mull of Kintyre, Girvan, Dumfries, Lockerbie, Hexham, NORTHERN IRELAND, Larne, Stranraer, Carlisle, ENGLAND, Hadrian's Wall, Wear, Carrickfergus, Solway Firth, Firth of Clyde, North Channel, West from Greenwich

Lewis, Harris, Outer Hebrides, Stornoway, North Uist, Benbecula, South Uist, Barra, Inner Hebrides, Rhum, Eigg, Mallaig, Coll, Tobermory, Tiree, Staffa, Mull, Iona, ATLANTIC OCEAN, Colonsay, Jura, Loch Fyne, Islay, Kintyre

NORTH SEA

**Shetland Islands** on same scale

Unst, Yell, Fetlar, Sullom Voe, Mainland, Foula, Lerwick

**Map scale**
This distance is 100 kilometres

COPYRIGHT PHILIP'S

26

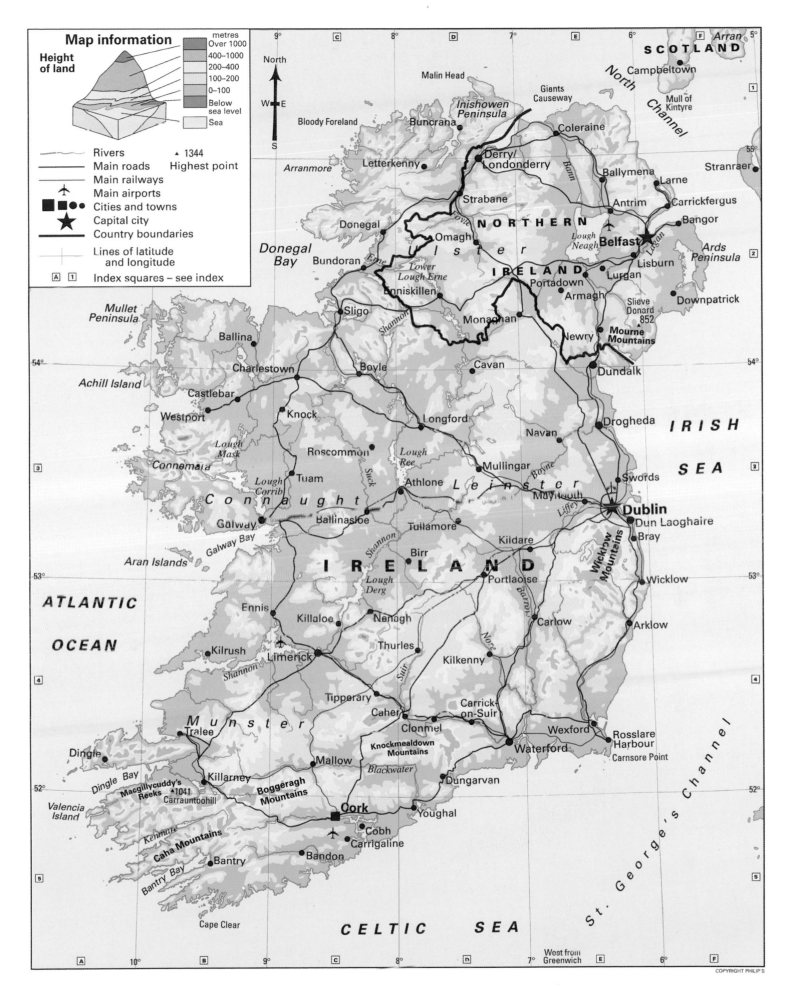

**Map information**

Height of land

metres
Over 1000
400–1000
200–400
100–200
0–100
Below sea level
Sea

Rivers
Main roads
Main railways
▲ 1344 Highest point
✈ Main airports
■ ▪ ▫ • Cities and towns
★ Capital city
Country boundaries
Lines of latitude and longitude
Ⓐ ① Index squares – see index

ATLANTIC OCEAN

SCOTLAND
Campbeltown
Mull of Kintyre
Arran
North Channel
Stranraer
Larne
Carrickfergus
Bangor
Ards Peninsula
Downpatrick

NORTHERN IRELAND
Malin Head
Inishowen Peninsula
Giants Causeway
Bloody Foreland
Buncrana
Coleraine
Letterkenny
Derry/Londonderry
Ballymena
Antrim
Strabane
Arranmore
Donegal
Omagh
Ulster
Belfast
Lisburn
Lurgan
Portadown
Armagh
Slieve Donard 852
Mourne Mountains
Newry
Lough Neagh
Bann
Lagan
Foyle
Erne

Donegal Bay
Bundoran
Lower Lough Erne
Enniskillen
Monaghan
Cavan
Dundalk
Drogheda

Mullet Peninsula
Ballina
Sligo
Shannon
Boyle
Longford
Navan
IRISH SEA

Achill Island
Charlestown
Castlebar
Westport
Knock
Roscommon
Lough Mask
Lough Ree
Mullingar
Boyne
Swords

Connemara
Lough Corrib
Tuam
Suck
Athlone
Leinster
Maynooth
Liffey
Dublin
Dun Laoghaire
Bray

Galway
Ballinasloe
IRELAND
Shannon
Tullamore
Kildare
Wicklow Mountains

Galway Bay
Aran Islands
Ennis
Killaloe
Birr
Lough Derg
Portlaoise
Barrow
Wicklow
Arklow

Limerick
Nenagh
Nore
Carlow

Kilrush
Shannon
Thurles
Kilkenny

Munster
Tipperary
Suir
Caher
Carrick-on-Suir
Wexford
Rosslare Harbour
Carnsore Point

Tralee
Dingle
Clonmel
Knockmealdown Mountains
Waterford

Macgillycuddy's Reeks ▲ 1041 Carrauntoohill
Killarney
Boggeragh Mountains
Mallow
Blackwater
Dungarvan

Valencia Island
Kenmare
Caha Mountains
Bantry
Bandon
Cork
Cobh
Carrigaline
Youghal

Dingle Bay
Bantry Bay
Cape Clear

CELTIC SEA

St. George's Channel

West from Greenwich

COPYRIGHT PHILIP'S

# The Earth as a planet

## Relative sizes of the planets

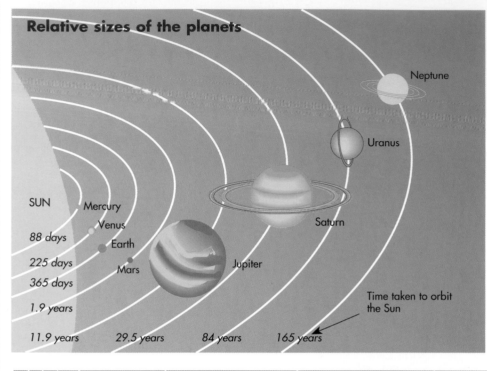

SUN

Mercury
Venus
Earth
Mars

Jupiter

Saturn

Uranus

Neptune

88 days

225 days

365 days

1.9 years

11.9 years     29.5 years     84 years     165 years

Time taken to orbit the Sun

### Distances of the planets from the Sun in millions of kilometres

Mercury 58
Venus 108   Earth 150
Mars 228
Jupiter 778
Saturn 1,430
Uranus 2,870
Neptune 4,500

## The Solar System

*The Earth is one of the eight planets that orbit the Sun. These two diagrams show how big the planets are, how far they are away from the Sun and how long they take to orbit the Sun. The diagram on the left shows how the planets closest to the Sun have the shortest orbits. The Earth takes 365 days (a year) to go round the Sun. The Earth is the fifth largest planet. It is much smaller than Jupiter and Saturn which are the largest planets.*

## Planet Earth

The Earth spins as if it is on a rod – its axis. The axis would come out of the Earth at two points. The northern point is called the North Pole and the southern point is called the South Pole. The distance between the Poles through the centre of the Earth is 12,700 km.

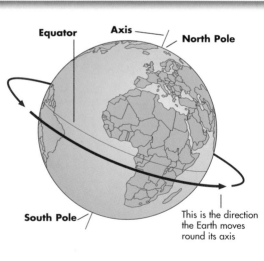

Equator    Axis    North Pole

South Pole

This is the direction the Earth moves round its axis

It takes a day (24 hours) for the Earth to rotate on its axis. It is light (day) when it faces the Sun and dark (night) when it faces away. See the diagram below. The Equator is a line round the Earth which is halfway between the Poles. It is 40,000 km long.

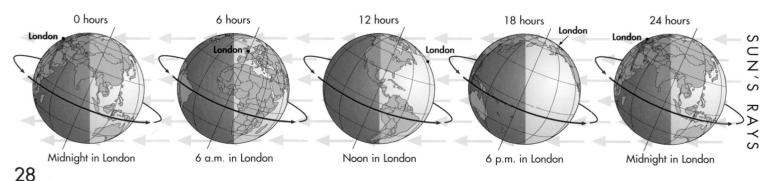

| 0 hours | 6 hours | 12 hours | 18 hours | 24 hours |
|---|---|---|---|---|
| London | London | London | London | London |
| Midnight in London | 6 a.m. in London | Noon in London | 6 p.m. in London | Midnight in London |

SUN'S RAYS

28

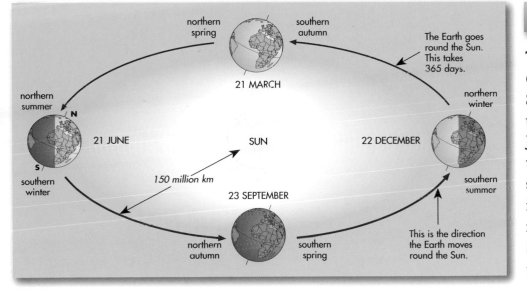

The Earth is always tilted at 66½°. It moves around the Sun. This movement gives us the seasons of the year. In June the northern hemisphere tilts towards the Sun so it is summer. Six months later, in December, the Earth has rotated halfway round the Sun. It is then summer in the southern hemisphere.

Sun's rays

**21 March**
Sun at right angles to tilt

**21 June**
In north, tilt towards the Sun

In south, tilt away from the Sun

**23 September**
Sun at right angles to tilt

**22 December**
In north, tilt away from the Sun

In south, tilt towards the Sun

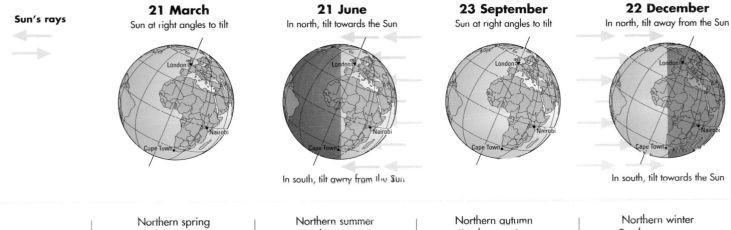

| Season | Northern spring Southern autumn | | | Northern summer Southern winter | | | Northern autumn Southern spring | | | Northern winter Southern summer | | |
|---|---|---|---|---|---|---|---|---|---|---|---|---|
| City | London | Nairobi | Cape Town | London | Nairobi | Cape Town | London | Nairobi | Cape Town | London | Nairobi | Cape Town |
| Latitude | 51°N | 1°S | 34°S | 51°N | 1°S | 34°S | 51°N | 1°S | 34°S | 51°N | 1°S | 34°S |
| Day length | 12 hrs | 12 hrs | 12 hrs | 16 hrs | 12 hrs | 10 hrs | 12 hrs | 12 hrs | 12 hrs | 8 hrs | 12 hrs | 14 hrs |
| Night length | 12 hrs | 12 hrs | 12 hrs | 8 hrs | 12 hrs | 14 hrs | 12 hrs | 12 hrs | 12 hrs | 16 hrs | 12 hrs | 10 hrs |
| Temperature | 7°C | 21°C | 21°C | 16°C | 18°C | 13°C | 15°C | 19°C | 14°C | 5°C | 19°C | 20°C |

## The Moon

*The Moon is about a quarter the size of the Earth. It orbits the Earth in just over 27 days (almost a month). The Moon is round but we on Earth see only the parts lit by the Sun. This makes it look as if the Moon is a different shape at different times of the month. These are known as the phases of the Moon and they are shown in this diagram.*

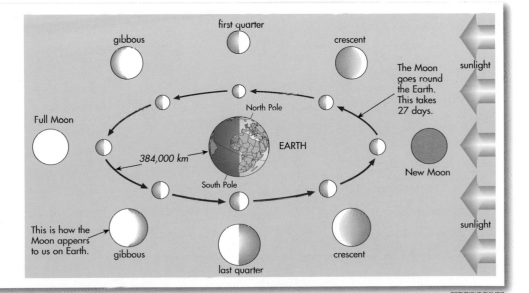

# Mountains, seas and rivers

Over 70% of the surface of the Earth is covered with water and ice. Most of the mountain ranges have been formed by movements in the Earth's crust. They are coloured brown on the map. Rivers shape the landscape as they flow to the sea.

## Largest oceans

*(thousand square kilometres)*

1. Pacific Ocean . . 155,557
2. Atlantic Ocean . . 76,762
3. Indian Ocean . . . 68,556
4. Southern Ocean . . 20,237
5. Arctic Ocean . . . 14,351

## Largest seas

*(thousand square kilometres)*

1. Mediterranean Sea  2,966
2. South China Sea   2,318
3. Bering Sea . . . . . . 2,274
4. Caribbean Sea . . . 1,942
5. Gulf of Mexico . . 1,813
6. Sea of Okhotsk . . 1,528

## Highest mountains

*(metres)*

Asia: Mt Everest . . . . 8,850

South America:
Aconcagua . . . . . . 6,962

North America:
Mt McKinley . . . 6,168

Africa: Kilimanjaro . . 5,895

Europe: Elbrus . . . . 5,642

## The course of a river

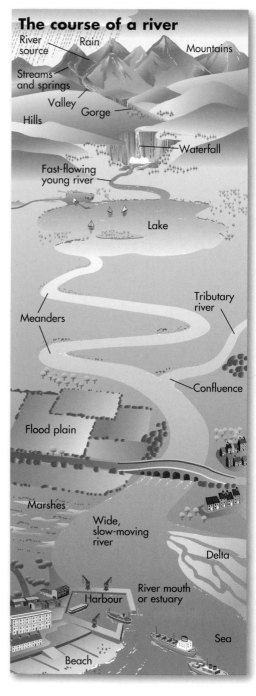

River source, Rain, Mountains, Streams and springs, Valley, Gorge, Hills, Waterfall, Fast-flowing young river, Lake, Meanders, Tributary river, Confluence, Flood plain, Marshes, Wide, slow-moving river, Delta, Harbour, River mouth or estuary, Sea, Beach

## Largest lakes

*(thousand square kilometres)*

| | |
|---|---|
| 1. Caspian Sea | 371 |
| 2. Lake Superior | 82 |
| 3. Lake Victoria | 68 |
| 4. Lake Huron | 60 |
| 5. Lake Michigan | 58 |
| 6. Lake Tanganyika | 33 |
| 7. Great Bear Lake | 32 |
| 8. Lake Baikal | 31 |
| 9. Lake Malawi | 30 |
| 10. Great Salt Lake | 29 |

## Longest rivers

*(kilometres)*

| | |
|---|---|
| 1. Nile | 6,695 |
| 2. Amazon | 6,450 |
| 3. Yangtse | 6,380 |
| 4. Mississippi | 5,971 |
| 5. Yenisey | 5,550 |
| 6. Hwang-Ho | 5,464 |
| 7. Ob | 5,410 |
| 8. Congo | 4,670 |
| 9. Mekong | 4,500 |
| 10. Amur | 4,442 |

## Largest islands

*(thousand square kilometres)*

| | |
|---|---|
| 1. Greenland | 2,176 |
| 2. New Guinea | 821 |
| 3. Borneo | 744 |
| 4. Madagascar | 587 |
| 5. Baffin Island | 508 |
| 6. Sumatra | 474 |
| 7. Honshu | 231 |
| 8. Great Britain | 230 |
| 9. Victoria Island | 212 |
| 10. Ellesmere Island | 197 |

## Deepest trenches

*(metres)*

| | |
|---|---|
| 1. Mariana Trench | 11,022 |
| 2. Tonga Trench | 10,822 |
| 3. Japan Trench | 10,554 |
| 4. Kuril Trench | 10,542 |
| 5. Mindanao Trench | 10,497 |
| 6. Kermadec Trench | 10,047 |
| 7. Bougainville Trench | 9,140 |
| 8. Milwaukee Deep | 8,605 |
| 9. South Sandwich Trench | 8,325 |
| 10. Aleutian Trench | 7,822 |

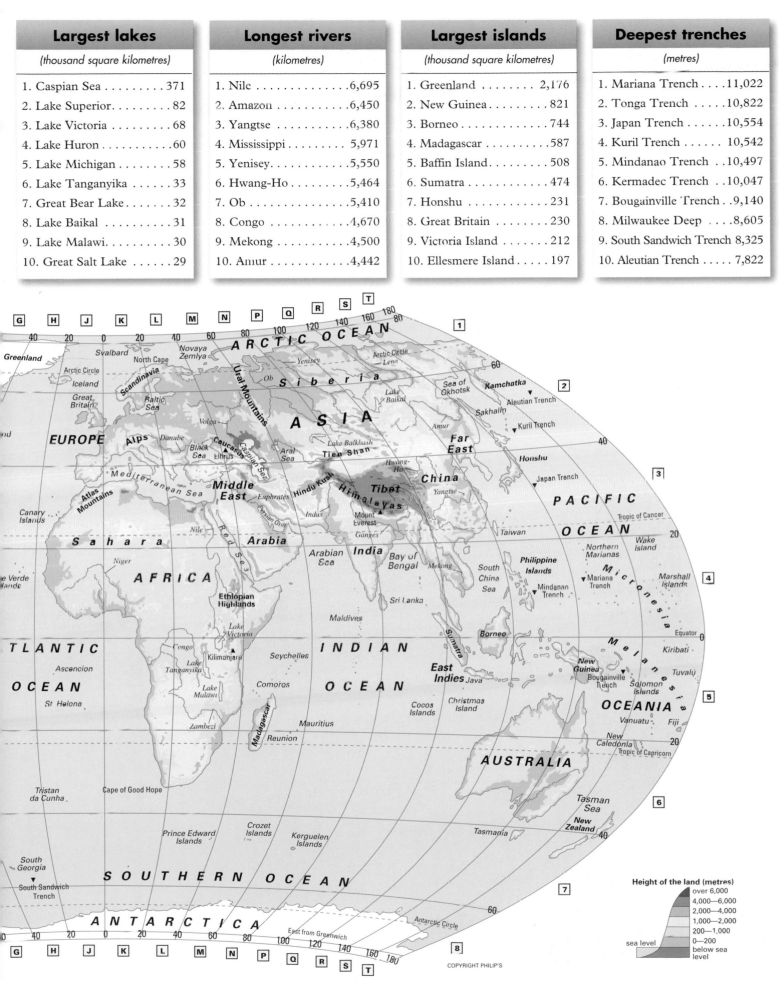

COPYRIGHT PHILIP'S

**Height of the land (metres)**
over 6,000
4,000—6,000
2,000—4,000
1,000—2,000
200—1,000
sea level
0—200
below sea level

# Climate

## Key to the climate map

**Tropical climate** (hot and wet)
Heavy rainfall and high temperatures all the year with little difference between the hot and cold months.

**Dry climate** (desert and steppe)
Many months, often years, without rain. High temperatures in the summer but cooler in winter.

**Mild climate** (warm and wet)
Rain every month. Warm summers and cool winters.

**Continental climate** (cold and wet)
Mild summers and very cold winters.

**Polar climate** (very cold and dry)
Very cold at all times, especially in the winter months. Very little rainfall.

**Mountainous areas** (where altitude affects climate type)
Lower temperatures because the land is high. Heavy rain and snow.

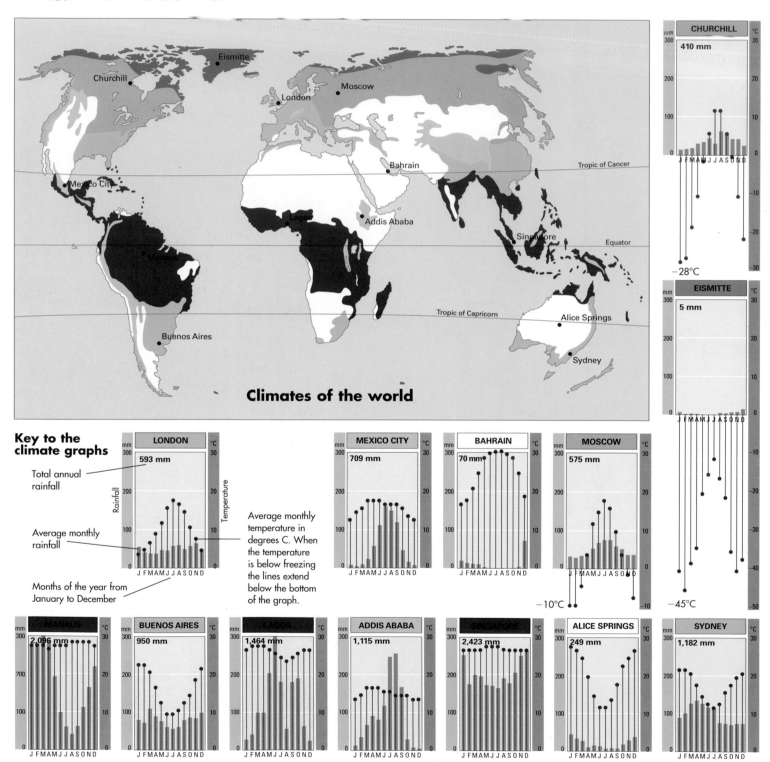

Climates of the world

## Key to the climate graphs

Total annual rainfall

Average monthly rainfall

Months of the year from January to December

Average monthly temperature in degrees C. When the temperature is below freezing the lines extend below the bottom of the graph.

## Annual rainfall

Human, plant and animal life cannot live without water. The map on the right shows how much rain falls in different parts of the world. You can see that there is a lot of rain in some places near the Equator. In other places, like the desert areas of the world, there is very little rain. Few plants or animals can survive there. There is also very little rain in the cold lands of the north.

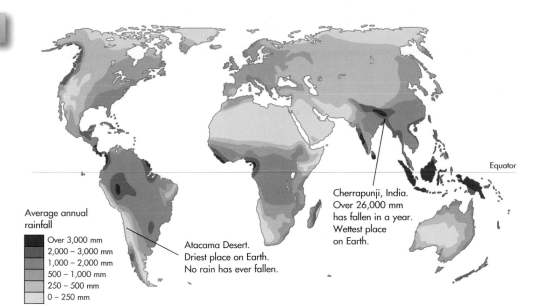

Average annual rainfall

Over 3,000 mm
2,000 – 3,000 mm
1,000 – 2,000 mm
500 – 1,000 mm
250 – 500 mm
0 – 250 mm

Equator

Cherrapunji, India. Over 26,000 mm has fallen in a year. Wettest place on Earth.

Atacama Desert. Driest place on Earth. No rain has ever fallen.

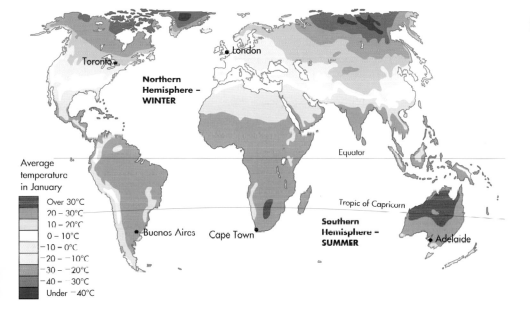

Toronto
London
Northern Hemisphere – WINTER
Equator
Tropic of Capricorn
Buenos Aires
Cape Town
Southern Hemisphere – SUMMER
Adelaide

Average temperature in January

Over 30°C
20 – 30°C
10 – 20°C
0 – 10°C
−10 – 0°C
−20 – −10°C
−30 – −20°C
−40 – −30°C
Under −40°C

## January temperature

In December, it is winter in the northern hemisphere. It is hot in the southern continents and cold in the northern continents. The North Pole is tilted away from the sun. It is overhead in the regions around the Tropic of Capricorn. This means that there are about 14 hours of daylight in Buenos Aires, Cape Town and Adelaide, and only about 8 hours in London and Toronto.

## July temperature

In July, it is summer in the northern hemisphere and winter in the southern hemisphere. It is warmer in the northern lands and colder in the south. The North Pole is tilted towards the sun. This means that in London and Toronto there are about 16 hours of daylight, but in Buenos Aires, Cape Town and Adelaide there are just under 10 hours.

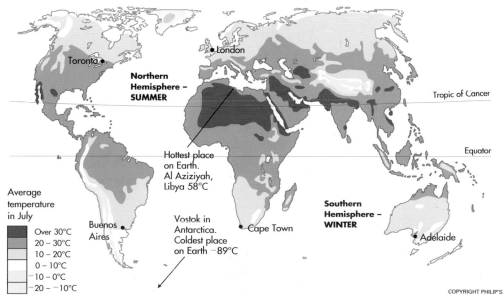

Toronto
London
Northern Hemisphere – SUMMER
Tropic of Cancer
Equator
Hottest place on Earth. Al Aziziyah, Libya 58°C
Buenos Aires
Vostok in Antarctica. Coldest place on Earth −89°C
Cape Town
Southern Hemisphere – WINTER
Adelaide

Average temperature in July

Over 30°C
20 – 30°C
10 – 20°C
0 – 10°C
−10 – 0°C
−20 – −10°C

COPYRIGHT PHILIP'S

33

# Climate change

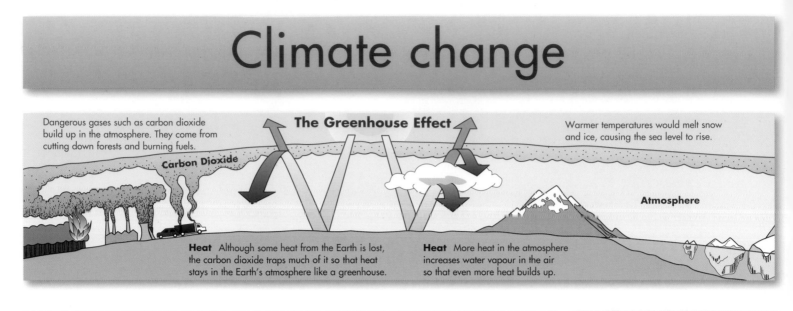

Dangerous gases such as carbon dioxide build up in the atmosphere. They come from cutting down forests and burning fuels.

**The Greenhouse Effect**

Warmer temperatures would melt snow and ice, causing the sea level to rise.

**Carbon Dioxide**

**Atmosphere**

**Heat** Although some heat from the Earth is lost, the carbon dioxide traps much of it so that heat stays in the Earth's atmosphere like a greenhouse.

**Heat** More heat in the atmosphere increases water vapour in the air so that even more heat builds up.

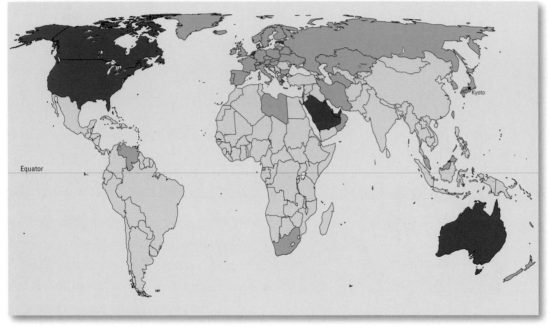

Equator

## Carbon dioxide

Major producers of carbon dioxide

Other producers of carbon dioxide

Countries producing very little carbon dioxide

This map shows which countries produce the most carbon dioxide per person. The countries that contribute the most to global warming tend to be rich countries like the USA and Australia. Can you think of reasons why?

## Global warming

Experts have studied climate data all around the world. They agreed several years ago that climate change really was happening. Leaders of all the major countries in the world came together in Kyoto in Japan to try and agree on what to do about it. This graph shows how temperatures might not rise as much if countries can cut their carbon dioxide emissions.

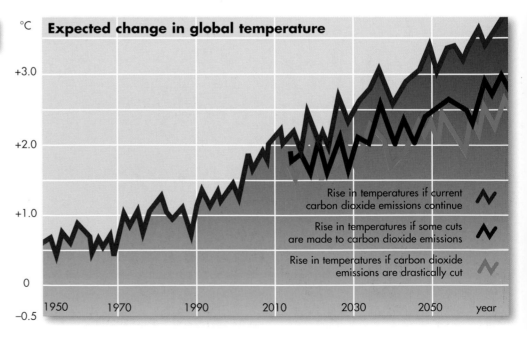

**Expected change in global temperature**

°C

+3.0

+2.0

+1.0

0

−0.5

1950    1970    1990    2010    2030    2050    year

Rise in temperatures if current carbon dioxide emissions continue

Rise in temperatures if some cuts are made to carbon dioxide emissions

Rise in temperatures if carbon dioxide emissions are drastically cut

## Temperature change

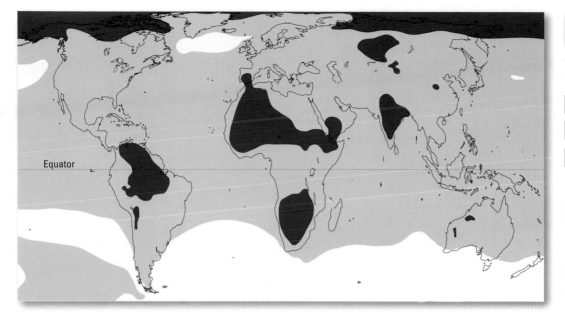

The expected change in temperature in the next 100 years

■ More than 5°C warmer

▨ Between 2°C and 5°C warmer

☐ Less than 2°C warmer

Compare this map with the map on the opposite page. The countries most affected by temperature change may not be the countries that are causing it.

## Rainfall change

The expected change in the amount of rainfall in the next 100 years

▨ More rainfall

☐ Very little change in the amount of rainfall

☐ Less rainfall

As the global climate changes, some parts of the world will get more rainfall, while other parts will become drier. Can you think of the effects this might have?

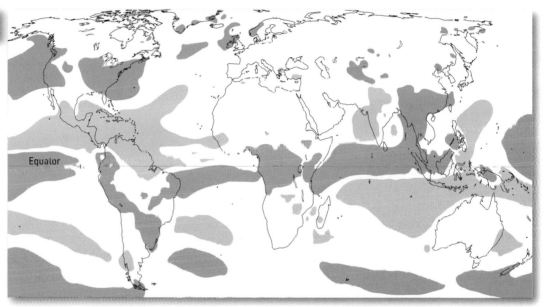

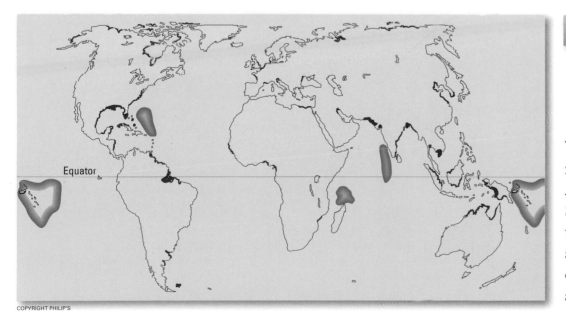

## Sea level rise

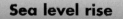
Areas at risk from rising sea level

Areas with many low-lying islands

Warmer temperatures will result in ice caps melting in Antarctica and Greenland. Sea levels will rise and threaten low-lying coastal areas and islands. Many of the world's largest cities are threatened.

# Forests, grasslands and wastes

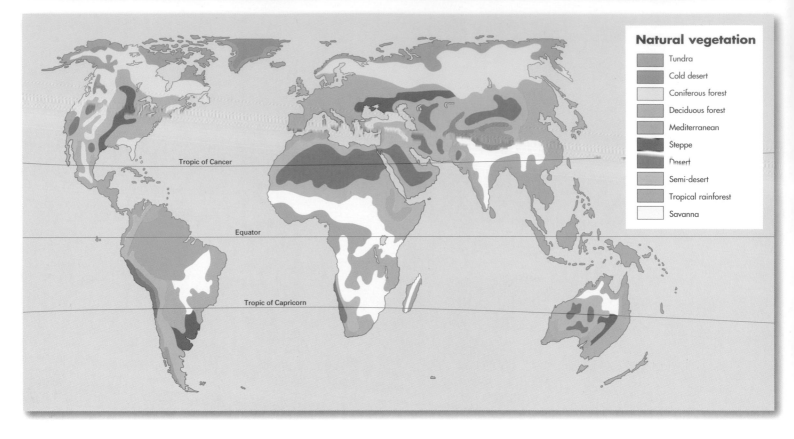

The map above shows types of vegetation. The diagram below shows the effect of altitude on types of vegetation.

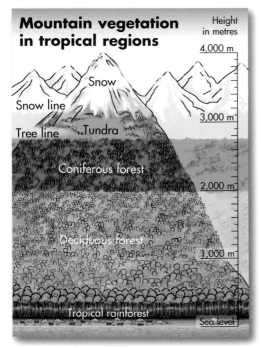

Mountain vegetation in tropical regions

Height in metres

4,000 m

Snow

Snow line

Tree line

Tundra

3,000 m

Coniferous forest

2,000 m

Deciduous forest

1,000 m

Tropical rainforest

Sea level

## Tundra
Long, dry, cold winters. Grasses, moss, bog and dwarf trees.

## Cold desert
Very cold with little rain or snow. No plants can grow.

## Coniferous forest
Harsh winters, mild summers. Trees have leaves all year.

## Deciduous forest
Rain all year, cool winters. Trees shed leaves in winter.

## Mediterranean
Hot, dry summers. Mild wet winters. Plants adapt to the heat.

## Steppe
Some rain with a dry season. Grasslands with some trees.

## Desert
Rain is rare. Plants only grow at oases with underground water.

## Semi-desert
Poor rains, sparse vegetation. Grass with a few small trees.

## Tropical rainforest (jungle)
Very hot and wet all the year. Tall trees and lush vegetation.

## Savanna
Mainly dry, but lush grass grows when the rains come.

## Tundra

Pingo (mound)

Thin, stony soil with permafrost below

Mosses, lichens and herbs

## Cold desert

No plants can grow

## Coniferous forest

*Evergreen conifers (spruces and firs)*

*Young tree saplings and small shrubs*

*Carpet of pine needles*

*Ferns and brambles on edge of forest*

## Yearly cycle of a deciduous forest

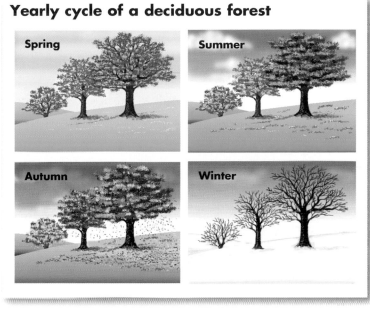

Spring

Summer

Autumn

Winter

## Mediterranean

Small stunted trees

Scrub

## Steppe

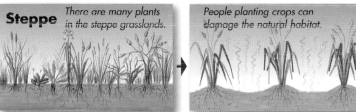

*There are many plants in the steppe grasslands.*

*People planting crops can damage the natural habitat.*

## Tropical rainforest

*Scattered trees with umbrella-shaped tops grow the highest.*

*Main layer of tall trees growing close together.*

*Creepers grow up the trees to reach the sunlight.*

*Ferns, mosses and small plants grow closest to the ground.*

## Desert

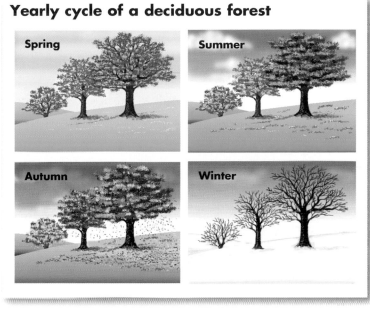

Cactus

Sand blown into dunes by the wind

Palm trees

Oasis

## Semi-desert

Joshua trees

Grass and bush

## Savanna

Dry season

Wet season

# Volcanoes and earthquakes

The Earth's crust is made up of a series of pieces called plates. The cracks between them are called plate boundaries. They are shown on the map below. In some areas the plates move towards each other and the heavier plate is forced under the lighter plate. If the plates rub together, the Earth's surface can be shaken backwards and forwards. Where the shaking is very destructive this is called an earthquake. Tsunami waves are caused by underwater earthquakes (see map opposite). When plates are forced down to great depths, they can melt to form magma. Volcanoes erupt when this magma is forced upwards to the surface.

| Major volcanic eruptions since 1900 | | |
|---|---|---|
| Year | Volcano | Deaths |
| 1902 | Mount Pelee, Martinique | 29,025 |
| 1902 | Soufriere, St. Vincent | 1,680 |
| 1902 | Santa Maria, Guatemala | 6,000 |
| 1911 | Taal, Philippines | 1,335 |
| 1919 | Kelud, Indonesia | 5,110 |
| 1951 | Mount Lamington, Papua New Guinea | 2,942 |
| 1963 | Agung, Indonesia | 1,184 |
| 1982 | El Chichon, Mexico | 2,000 |
| 1985 | Nevado del Ruiz, Colombia | 25,000 |
| 1986 | Lake Nyos, Cameroon | 1,700 |
| 1991 | Pinatubo, Philippines | 800 |

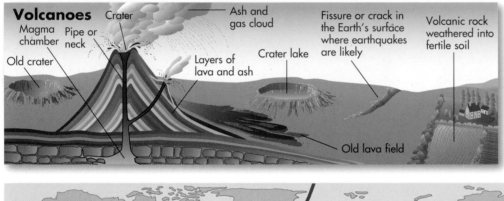

**Volcanoes** — Crater, Magma chamber, Pipe or neck, Old crater, Ash and gas cloud, Layers of lava and ash, Crater lake, Fissure or crack in the Earth's surface where earthquakes are likely, Volcanic rock weathered into fertile soil, Old lava field

Volcanic regions

△ Volcanoes (active since 1700)

1991 Year of major volcanic eruptions since 1900

— Plate boundaries

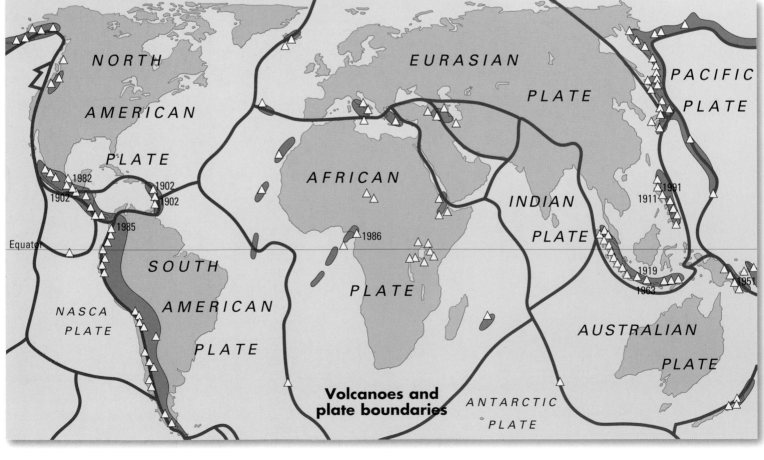

**Volcanoes and plate boundaries**

NORTH AMERICAN PLATE · EURASIAN PLATE · PACIFIC PLATE · AFRICAN PLATE · INDIAN PLATE · SOUTH AMERICAN PLATE · NASCA PLATE · AUSTRALIAN PLATE · ANTARCTIC PLATE · Equator

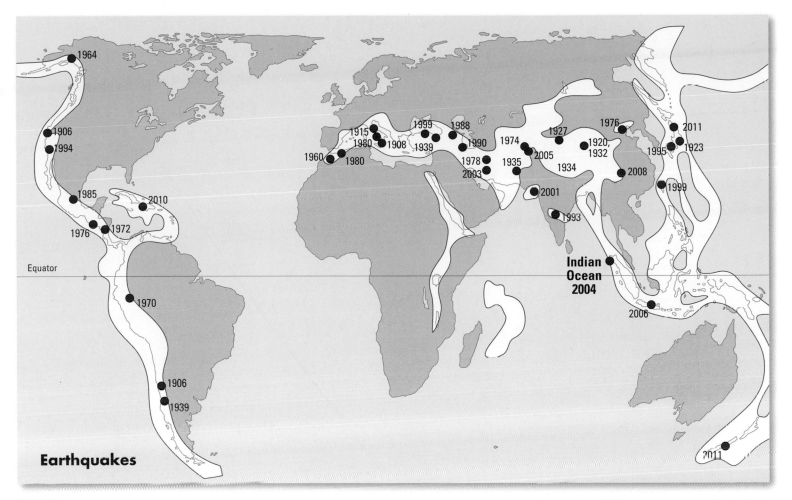

**Earthquakes**

Earthquake regions

● Major earthquakes since 1900 with dates

| Major earthquakes since 1900 | | | |
|---|---|---|---|
| *Year* | *Location* | *Magnitude* | *Deaths* |
| 1908 | Messina, Italy | 7.5 | 83,000 |
| 1915 | Avezzano, Italy | 7.5 | 30,000 |
| 1920 | Gansu, China | 8.6 | 180,000 |
| 1923 | Yokohama, Japan | 8.3 | 143,000 |
| 1927 | Nan Shan, China | 8.3 | 200,000 |
| 1932 | Gansu, China | 7.6 | 70,000 |
| 1970 | Northern Peru | 7.8 | 66,794 |
| 1976 | Tangshan, China | 8.2 | 255,000 |
| 1988 | Armenia | 6.8 | 55,000 |
| 1993 | Maharashtra, India | 6.4 | 30,000 |
| 1995 | Kobe, Japan | 7.2 | 5,000 |
| 2001 | Gujarat, India | 7.7 | 14,000 |
| 2003 | Bam, Iran | 7.1 | 30,000 |
| 2004 | Sumatra, Indonesia | 9.0 | 230,000 |
| 2005 | Northern Pakistan | 7.6 | 74,000 |
| 2008 | Sichuan, China | 7.9 | 70,000 |
| 2010 | Haiti | 7.0 | 230,000 |
| 2011 | Northern Japan | 9.0 | 22,600 |

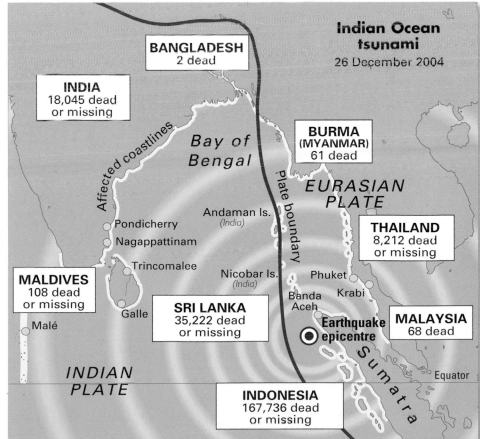

**Indian Ocean tsunami**
26 December 2004

BANGLADESH
2 dead

INDIA
18,045 dead or missing

BURMA (MYANMAR)
61 dead

*Bay of Bengal*

EURASIAN PLATE

THAILAND
8,212 dead or missing

MALDIVES
108 dead or missing

Andaman Is. *(India)*

Pondicherry
Nagappattinam
Trincomalee

Nicobar Is. *(India)*

Phuket
Krabi
Banda Aceh

Galle

SRI LANKA
35,222 dead or missing

*Affected coastlines*

*Plate boundary*

Male

Earthquake epicentre

MALAYSIA
68 dead

INDIAN PLATE

INDONESIA
167,736 dead or missing

*Sumatra*

Equator

# Farming and fishing

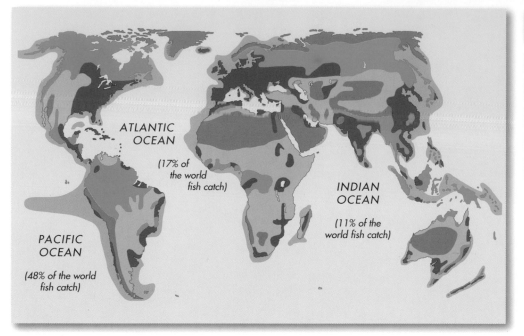

ATLANTIC
OCEAN

*(17% of
the world
fish catch)*

INDIAN
OCEAN

*(11% of
the world fish catch)*

PACIFIC
OCEAN

*(48% of the world
fish catch)*

## How the land is used

Forest areas with timber. Some hunting and fishing. Some farming in the tropics.

Deserts and wastelands

Animal farming on large farms (ranches)

Farming of crops and animals on large and small farms

Main fishing areas

Deserts and wastelands cover 32% of the world's total land area. Forests cover a further 30%. What percentage of the total land area does that leave for the farming of crops and animals?

## The importance of agriculture

Over half the people work in agriculture

Between a quarter and half the people work in agriculture

Between one in ten and a quarter of the people work in agriculture

Less than one in ten of the people work in agriculture

A hundred years ago about 80% of the world's population worked in agriculture. Today it is only about 30% but agriculture is still very important in some countries.

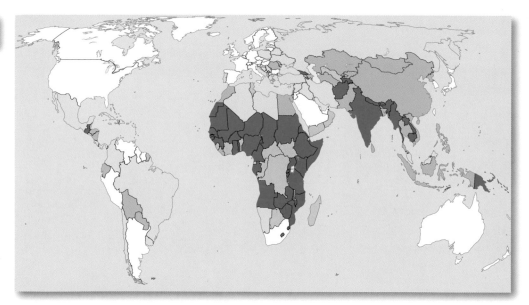

## Methods of fishing

There are two types of sea fishing:

1. **Deep-sea fishing** using large trawlers which often stay at sea for many weeks.

2. **Inshore fishing** using small boats, traps and nets up to 70 km from the coast.

**Inshore fishing**

Lobster pots

Fish trap

Sonar is used to find fish

**Deep-sea fishing** (drifter)

Fishing vessels (trawler)

Seine net to catch herring, tuna and mackerel

Trawl net to catch fish near the sea bed (sole, cod and haddock)

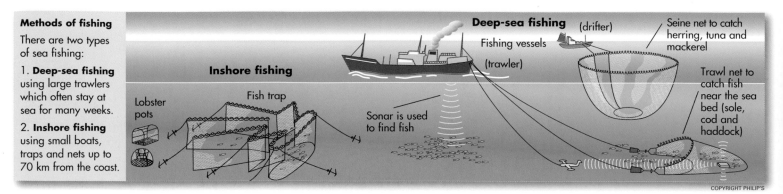

# Energy resources

## Oil and gas resources

 Oilfields

Natural gasfields

→ Main routes for transporting oil and gas by tanker

Crude oil is drilled from deep in the Earth's crust. The oil is then refined so that it can be used in different industries. Oil is used to make petrol and is also very important in the chemical industry. Natural gas is often found in the same places as oil.

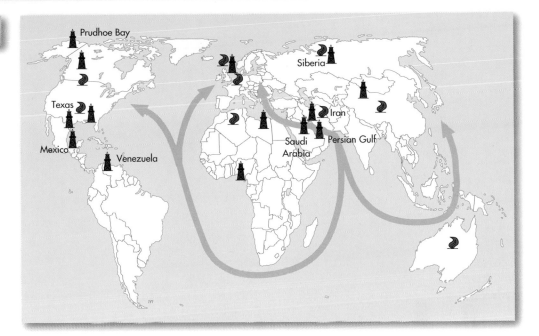

## Coal resources

▲ Hard coal (bituminous)

▲ Lignite (soft brown coal)

→ Main routes for transporting coal

Coal is a fuel that comes from forests and swamps that rotted millions of years ago and have been crushed by layers of rock. The coal is cut out of the rock from deep mines and also from open-cast mines where the coal is nearer the surface. The oldest type of coal is hard. The coal formed more recently is softer.

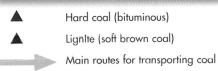

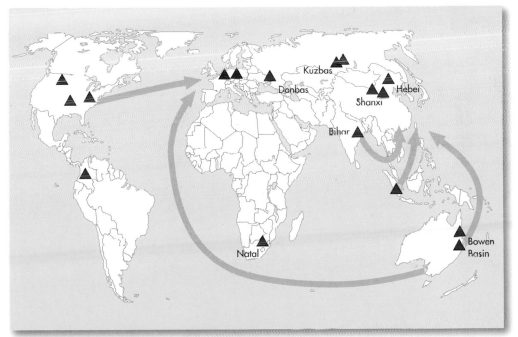

## Renewable resources

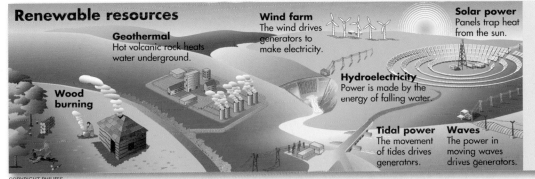

**Wood burning**

**Geothermal**
Hot volcanic rock heats water underground.

**Wind farm**
The wind drives generators to make electricity.

**Solar power**
Panels trap heat from the sun.

**Hydroelectricity**
Power is made by the energy of falling water.

**Tidal power**
The movement of tides drives generators.

**Waves**
The power in moving waves drives generators.

Oil, gas and coal are all resources which provide energy. Once these resources have been used up, they cannot be replaced. They are called **non-renewable resources**.

Energy is also provided by the sun, wind, waves, tides, and hot water from deep in the Earth. These resources will never run out. They are called **renewable resources**.

# Transport and tourism

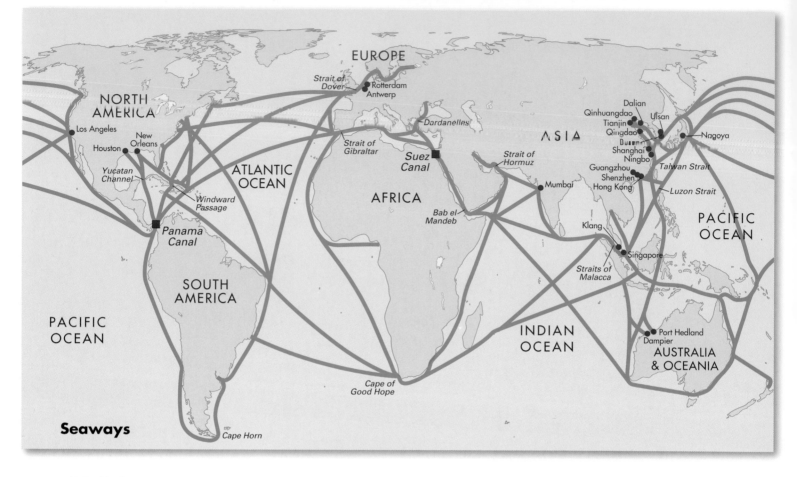

Seaways

— Main shipping routes

● The biggest seaports in the world

Sea transport is used for goods that are too bulky or heavy to go by air or land. The main shipping routes are between North America, Europe and the Far East.

## Panama Canal and Suez Canal

These two important canals cut through narrow pieces of land. Can you work out how much shorter the journeys are by using the canals?

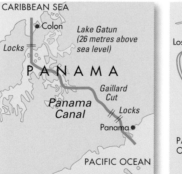

## Panama Canal

- Opened in 1914
- 82 km long
- 13,000 ships a year
- Average toll $54,000
- Locks are needed in the Panama Canal to go between the Caribbean Sea and the Pacific Ocean

## Suez Canal

- Opened in 1870
- 162 km long
- 21,000 ships a year
- Average toll $250,000
- The Suez Canal has no locks between the Mediterranean Sea and the Red Sea

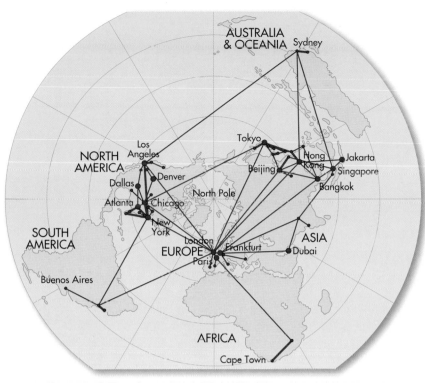

## Airways

This map has the North Pole at its centre. It shows how much air traffic connects Europe, North America and Eastern Asia. You can see the long distances in the USA and Asia that are covered by air.

- ● Large international airports (over 50 million passengers a year)
- · Other important airports
- ▬ Heavily used air routes
- — Other important air routes

## Tourism

In 2012 there were 1,035 billion tourists visiting foreign countries. The most popular country to visit was France, followed by the USA, China and Spain.

- □ Ski resorts
- ■ Centres of entertainment
- ■ Cultural and historical centres
- ■ Places of pilgrimage
- ■ Places of great natural beauty
- □ Coastal resorts

### Air distances (kilometres)

|  | Buenos Aires | Cape Town | London | Los Angeles | New York | Sydney | Tokyo |
|---|---|---|---|---|---|---|---|
| Buenos Aires |  | 6,880 | 11,128 | 9,854 | 8,526 | 11,760 | 18,338 |
| Cape Town | 6,880 |  | 9,672 | 16,067 | 12,551 | 10,982 | 14,710 |
| London | 11,128 | 9,672 |  | 8,752 | 5,535 | 17,005 | 9,584 |
| Los Angeles | 9,854 | 16,067 | 8,752 |  | 3,968 | 12,052 | 8,806 |
| New York | 8,526 | 12,551 | 5,535 | 3,968 |  | 16,001 | 10,869 |
| Sydney | 11,760 | 10,982 | 17,005 | 12,052 | 16,001 |  | 7,809 |
| Tokyo | 18,338 | 14,710 | 9,584 | 8,806 | 10,869 | 7,809 |  |

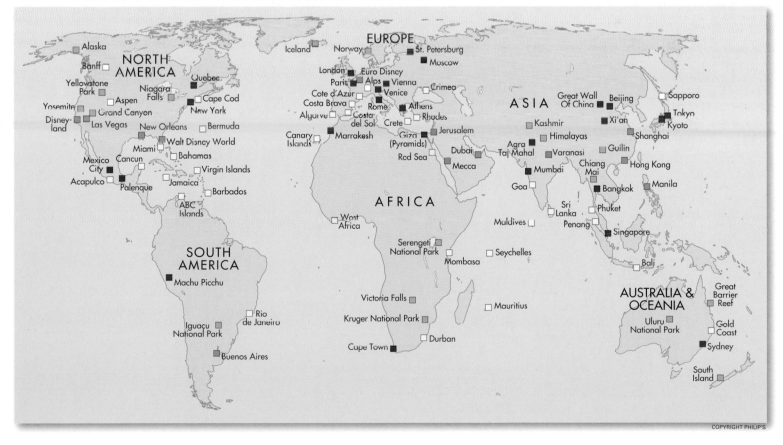

# Rich and poor

All countries have both rich and poor people but some countries have more poor people than others. The amount of food that people have to eat and the age that they die can often depend on where they live in the world. The world can be divided into two parts – the rich and the poor.

The rich countries are mostly in the North and the poor countries are mostly in the South. The map below shows which countries are rich and which are poor. The list on the right shows some contrasts between rich and poor. Some of these contrasts can be seen in the maps on these pages.

| **Rich** | **Poor** |
|---|---|
| • Good health | • Poor health |
| • Well educated | • Poorly educated |
| • Well fed | • Poorly fed |
| • Small families | • Large families |
| • Many industries | • Few industries |
| • Few farmers | • Many farmers |
| • Give aid | • Receive aid |

Poor countries have over three-quarters of the world's population but less than a quarter of its wealth.

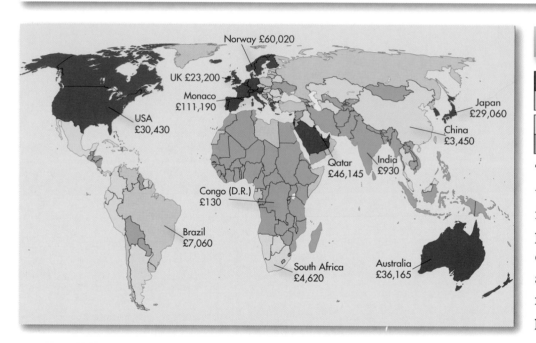

## Income

| | |
|---|---|
| ■ | Very rich countries |
| ■ | Rich countries |
| ■ | Poor countries |
| ■ | Very poor countries |

The map shows how much money there is to spend on each person in a country. This is called income per person – this is worked out by dividing the wealth of a country by its population. The map gives examples of rich and poor countries.

Map labels: Norway £60,020; UK £23,200; Monaco £111,190; USA £30,430; Japan £29,060; China £3,450; Qatar £46,145; India £930; Congo (D.R.) £130; Brazil £7,060; South Africa £4,620; Australia £36,165

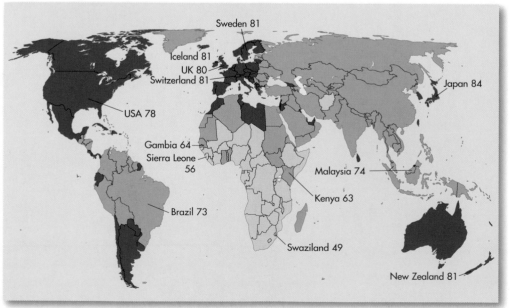

## How long do people live?

This is the average age when people die

| | |
|---|---|
| ■ | Over 75 years |
| ■ | 60 – 75 years |
| ■ | Under 60 years |

The average age of death is called life expectancy. In the world as a whole, the average life expectancy is 68 years. Some of the highest and lowest ages of death are shown on the map.

Map labels: Sweden 81; Iceland 81; UK 80; Switzerland 81; Japan 84; USA 78; Gambia 64; Sierra Leone 56; Malaysia 74; Kenya 63; Brazil 73; Swaziland 49; New Zealand 81

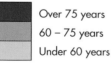

## Food and famine

- Below the amount of food they need
- Above the amount of food they need
- Over a third above the amount of food they need

★ Major famines since 1980

If people do not have enough to eat they become unhealthy. This map shows where in the world people have less than and more than the amount of food they need to live a healthy life.

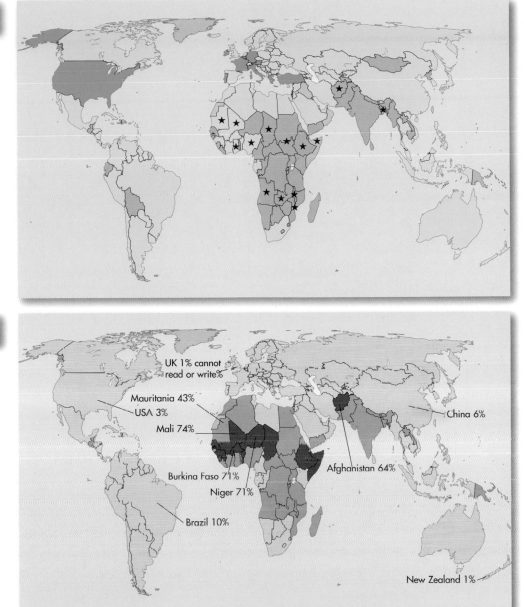

## Reading and writing

- Over half the adults cannot read or write
- Between a quarter and a half of the adults cannot read or write
- Less than a quarter of the adults cannot read or write

The map shows the proportion of adults in each country who cannot read or write a simple sentence. Can you think of some reasons why more people cannot read or write in some places in the world than in others?

UK 1% cannot read or write%

Mauritania 43%

USA 3%

Mali 74%

China 6%

Burkina Faso 71%

Niger 71%

Afghanistan 64%

Brazil 10%

New Zealand 1%

## Development aid

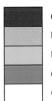

- Over £25 received per person each year
- Up to £25 received per person each year
- Up to £100 given per person each year
- Over £100 given per person each year
- Countries that receive or give no aid

Some countries receive aid from other countries. Money is one type of aid. It is used to help with food, health and education problems. The map shows how much different countries give or receive.

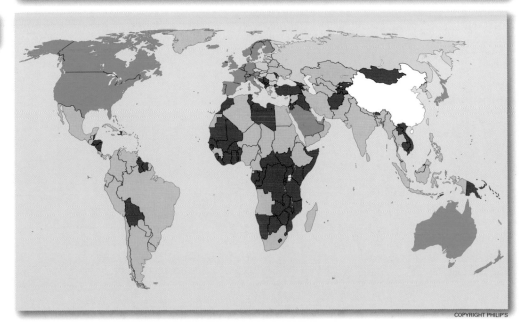

45

# Peoples and cities

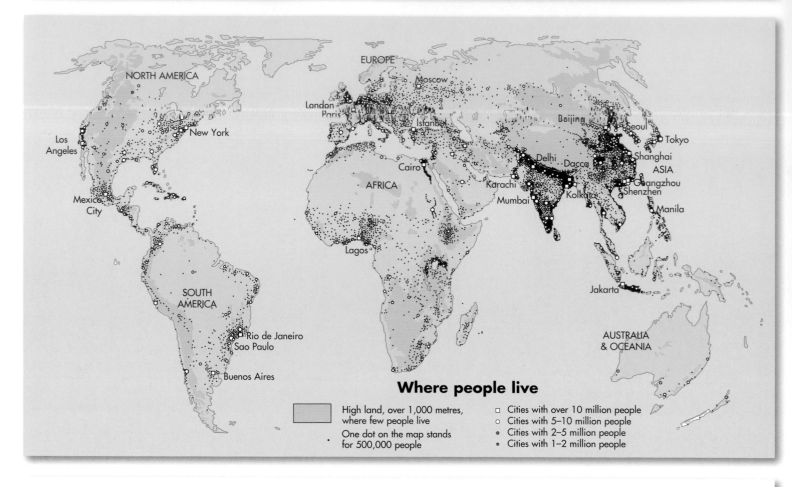

## Where people live

High land, over 1,000 metres, where few people live

- One dot on the map stands for 500,000 people

- □ Cities with over 10 million people
- ○ Cities with 5–10 million people
- ● Cities with 2–5 million people
- • Cities with 1–2 million people

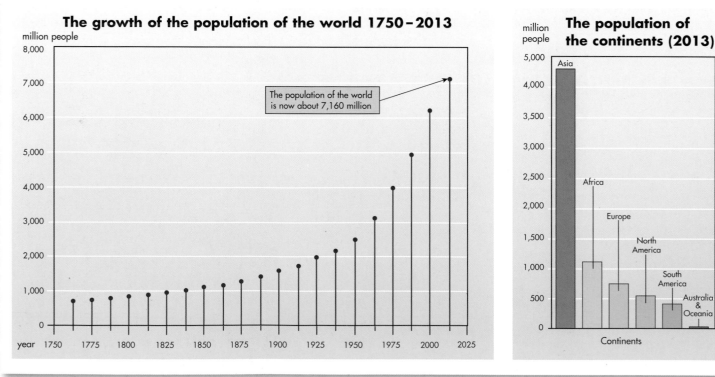

### The growth of the population of the world 1750–2013

million people

The population of the world is now about 7,160 million

### The population of the continents (2013)

million people

Continents

## Largest nations

(population of countries in millions)

1. China . . . . . . . . 1,343
2. India . . . . . . . . . 1,205
3. USA . . . . . . . . . 314
4. Indonesia. . . . . . . 248
5. Brazil. . . . . . . . . 206
6. Pakistan. . . . . . . 190
7. Nigeria . . . . . . . 170
8. Bangladesh . . . . . 161
9. Russia . . . . . . . . 138
10. Japan. . . . . . . . . 127
11. Mexico . . . . . . . 115
12. Philippines. . . . . . 104
13. Ethiopia. . . . . . . . 94
14. Vietnam. . . . . . . . 92
15. Egypt. . . . . . . . . 84
16. Germany . . . . . . . 81
17. Turkey . . . . . . . . 80
18. Iran. . . . . . . . . . 79
19. Congo (Dem. Rep.) 74
20. Thailand . . . . . . . 67
21. France. . . . . . . . 66
22. UK . . . . . . . . . . 63

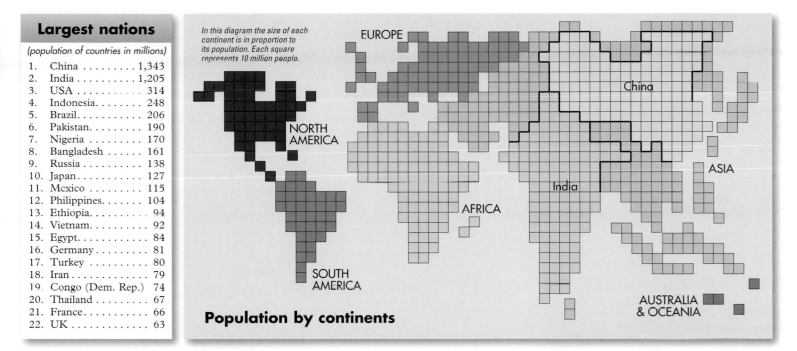

In this diagram the size of each continent is in proportion to its population. Each square represents 10 million people.

### Population by continents

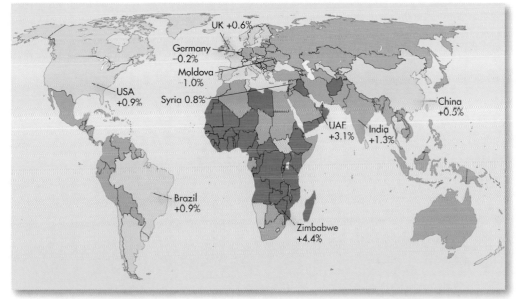

## Increase and decrease

### Annual rate of change in 2012

- Over 2% gain in the number of people
- Between 1% and 2% gain
- Under 1% gain
- Loss in the number of people

The map shows the rate of change in the number of people in each country. The largest increases are in poor countries in Africa and Asia. The number of people living in some richer countries is decreasing.

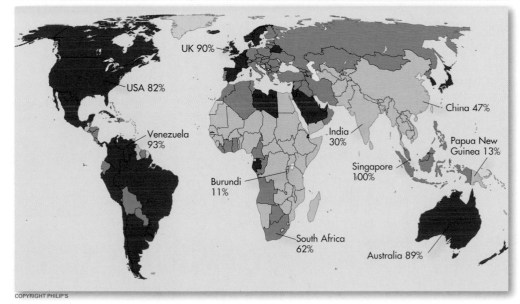

## Living in cities

### Urban population as a percentage of the total population

- Over three-quarters of the population live in cities
- Between a half and three-quarters live in cities
- Less than half live in cities

In 2008, for the first time in history, more than half of the world's population lived in cities. Why do you think people move from farms and villages to towns and cities?

47

# Countries of the world

## North America

*(see pages 58–59)*

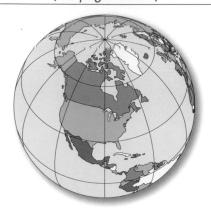

## South America

*(see pages 60–61)*

## Africa

*(see pages 54–55)*

These pages show different maps of the world. The large map shows the world cut through the Pacific Ocean and opened out on to flat paper. The smaller maps of the continents are views of the globe looking down on each of the continents.

Larger maps of the continents appear on the following pages. They show more cities than on this map.

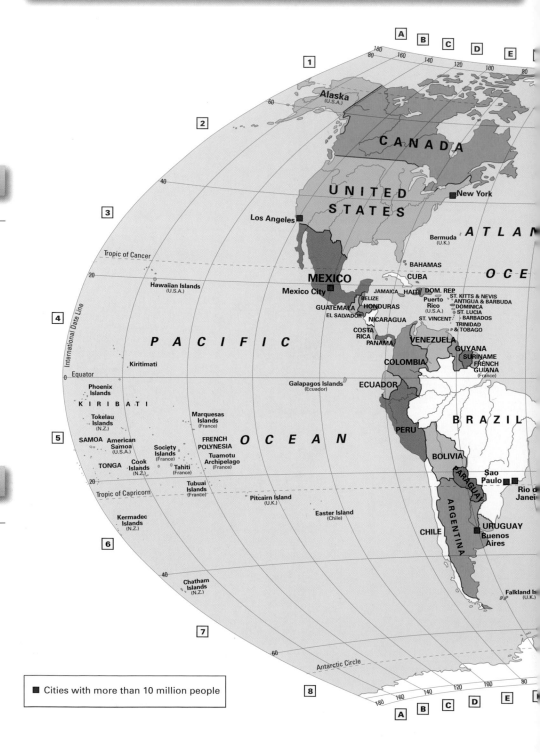

■ Cities with more than 10 million people

48

## Europe
(see pages 50–51)

## Asia
(see pages 52–53)

## Oceania
(see pages 56–57)

| ALB. | = Albania | LUX. | = Luxembourg |
|------|-----------|------|--------------|
| ARM. | = Armenia | MAC. | = Macedonia |
| AZER. | = Azerbaijan | M. | = Montenegro |
| BELG. | = Belgium | NETH. | = Netherlands |
| B.-H. | = Bosnia-Herzegovina | S. | = Serbia |
| CR. | = Croatia | SLO. | = Slovenia |
| CZECH. | = Czech Republic | SWITZ. | = Switzerland |
| DOM. REP. | = Dominican Republic | U.A.E. | = United Arab Emirates |
| K. | = Kosovo | U.K. | = United Kingdom |
| LEB. | = Lebanon | U.S.A. | = United States of America |

COPYRIGHT PHILIP'S

# Europe

## Largest countries – by area
### (thousand square kilometres)

1. Russia ..................... 17,075
2. Ukraine ..................... 604
3. France ..................... 552
4. Spain ..................... 498

## Largest countries – by population
### (million people)

1. Russia ............. 138
2. Germany ........... 81
3. France ............ 66
4. United Kingdom ..... 63

## Largest cities
### (million people)

1. Moscow (RUSSIA) ..... 11.6
2. Istanbul (TURKEY) ..... 11.3
3. Paris (FRANCE) ....... 10.6
4. London (UK) ........ 9.0

- ■ Europe is the second smallest continent. It is one-fifth the size of Asia. Australia is slightly smaller than Europe.
- ■ The Ural Mountains form the eastern boundary of Europe.
- ■ Great Britain is the largest island in Europe.

### Height of the land (metres)
- over 4,000
- 2,000 – 4,000
- 1,000 – 2,000
- 400 – 1,000
- 200 – 400
- 0 – 200
- sea level
- below sea level

**Map scale**
This distance is 1,000 kilometres

ARCTIC OCEAN

North Cape

**Map information**
- ■●● Cities
- ★ Capital city
- Ⓐ Index square - see index
- ——— Country boundary
- ▨ Sea and lakes

**Map scale**
This distance is 750 kilometres

Murmansk

Lofoten
Islands

Narvik

Arctic Circle

White
Sea

Arkhangelsk

North Dvina

Perm

Trondheim

Gulf of Bothnia

N
O
R
W
A
Y

S
W
E
D
E
N

F
I
N
L
A
N
D

Lake Onega

Lake Ladoga

Yekaterinburg

Shetland
Islands
(U.K.)

Bergen

Oslo

Stockholm

Helsinki

St. Petersburg

Volga

Ufa

R  U  S  S  I  A

Gothenburg

Tallinn

**ESTONIA**

Kazan

Samara

North
Sea

Baltic Sea

Gulf of Finland

Riga

**LATVIA**

MOSCOW

**DENMARK**
Copenhagen

**LITHUANIA**

KALININGRAD
(Russia)

Vilnius

Voronezh

Ural

Caspian Sea

Gdansk

Minsk

**BELARUS**

Hamburg

Vistula

THERLANDS
Amsterdam
The Hague

Berlin

Warsaw

Elbe

ssels

**GERMANY**

**POLAND**

Kiev

Kharkov

Volgograd

Don

Volga

ELGIUM

**LUXEMBOURG**

Frankfurt

Oder

Lvov

**U  K  R  A  I  N  E**

Donetsk

Luxembourg

**CZECH
REPUBLIC**

Prague

Krakow

Rhine

Munich

**SLOVAK
REPUBLIC**

Dnepropetrovsk

Rostov

Bern

Vienna

Bratislava

**MOLDOVA**

LIECHTEN-
STEIN

**AUSTRIA**

Budapest

Kishinev

Odessa

Sea of
Azov

Krasnodar

ons

SWITZERLAND

**HUNGARY**

Ljubljana

**SLOVENIA**

Zagreb

**CROATIA**

**ROMANIA**

Crimea

Milan

Turin

**I
T
A
L
Y**

Adriatic Sea

**BOSNIA-
HERZEGOVINA**

Belgrade

Bucharest

Danube

Sevastopol

Black  Sea

MONACO

SAN
MARINO

Sarajevo

**SERBIA**

rseilles

Podgorica

**KOSOVO**

Sofia

Corsica
(France)

**MONTENEGRO**

Pristina

**BULGARIA**

Rome

Skopje

Istanbul

dinia
aly)

Naples

Tirane

**MACEDONIA**

**ALBANIA**

Ankara

**G  R  E  E  C  E**

**T  U  R  K  E  Y**

A  S  I  A

rranean

Palermo

Sicily

Aegean
Sea

Izmir

Athens

Sea

Crete

Nicosia

Valletta

**MALTA**

**CYPRUS**

COPYRIGHT PHILIP'S

North
W E
S

51

# Asia

## Largest countries – by area

*(thousand square kilometres)*

1. Russia . . . . . . . . . . . 17,075
2. China . . . . . . . . . . . 9,597
3. India . . . . . . . . . . . 3,287

## Largest countries – by population

*(million people)*

1. China . . . . . . . . . . . 1,343
2. India . . . . . . . . . . . 1,205
3. Indonesia . . . . . . . . . 248
4. Pakistan . . . . . . . . . . 190

## Largest cities

*(million people)*

1. Tokyo (JAPAN) . . . . . . . 37.2
2. Delhi (INDIA) . . . . . . . 22.7
3. Shanghai (CHINA) . . . . . 20.2
4. Mumbai (INDIA) . . . . . . 19.7
5. Beijing (CHINA) . . . . . . 15.6

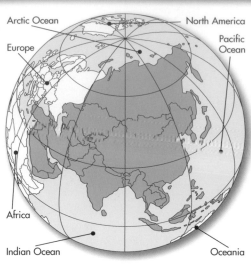

- Asia is the largest continent. It is twice the size of North America.
- It is a continent of long rivers. Many of Asia's rivers are longer than Europe's longest river.
- Asia contains well over half of the world's population.

## Map information

- ■●• Cities
- ★ Capital city
- Ⓐ Index square - see index
- —— Country boundary
- ▢ Sea and lakes

### Map scale

This distance is 2,000 kilometres

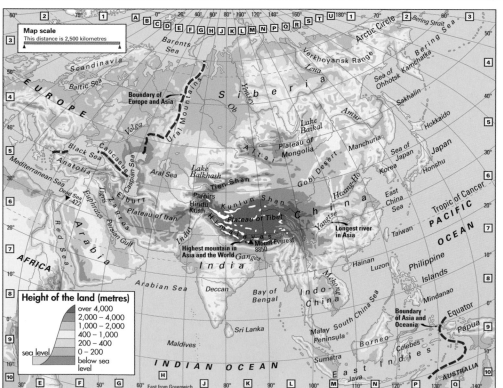

**Map scale**
This distance is 2,500 kilometres

**Height of the land (metres)**

- over 4,000
- 2,000 – 4,000
- 1,000 – 2,000
- 400 – 1,000
- 200 – 400
- 0 – 200
- below sea level

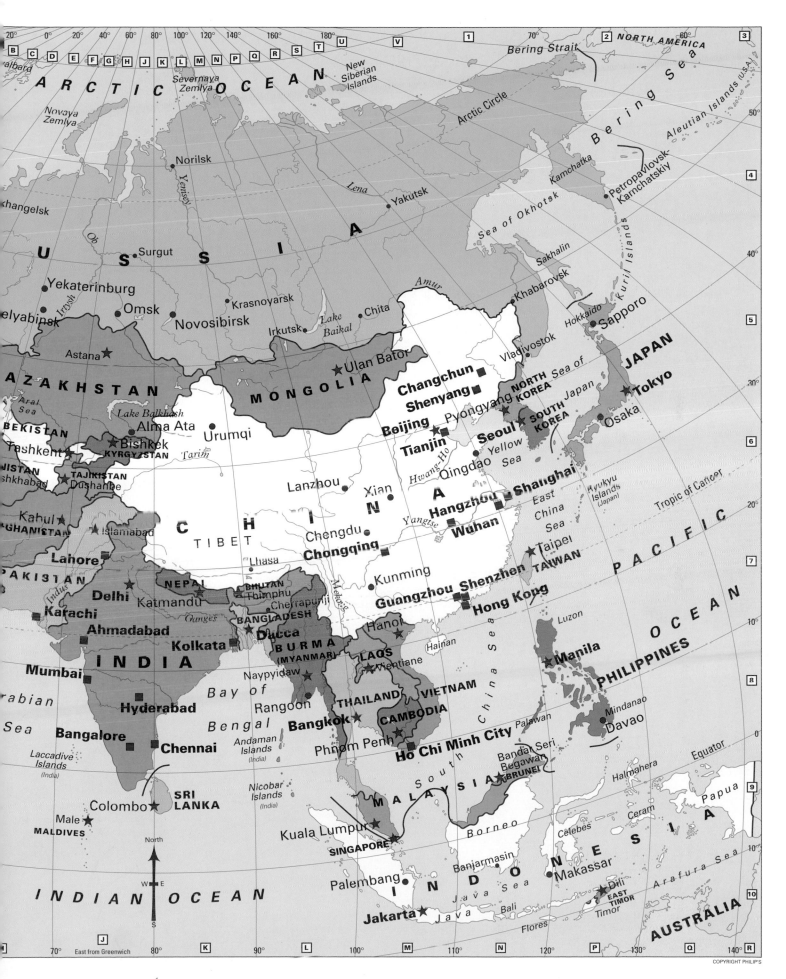

ARCTIC OCEAN

Bering Strait

NORTH AMERICA

Bering Sea

Aleutian Islands (U.S.A.)

Severnaya Zemlya

New Siberian Islands

Novaya Zemlya

Arctic Circle

Norilsk

Yenisey

Lena

Yakutsk

Sea of Okhotsk

Kamchatka

Petropavlovsk-Karnchatskiy

Kuril Islands

Surgut

Khabarovsk

Sakhalin

Hokkaido

Sapporo

U S S I A

Yekaterinburg

Ob

Irtysh

Omsk

Krasnoyarsk

Novosibirsk

Irkutsk

Lake Baikal

Chita

Amur

Vladivostok

JAPAN

Tokyo

elyabinsk

khangelsk

Astana

Ulan Bator

MONGOLIA

Changchun

Shenyang

Sea of Japan

NORTH KOREA

Osaka

AZAKHSTAN

Lake Balkhash

Alma Ata

Urumqi

Beijing

Pyongyang

Aral Sea

Tianjin

Seoul

SOUTH KOREA

BEKISTAN

Bishkek

KYRGYZSTAN

Tarim

Qingdao

Yellow Sea

Hwang-Ho

ashkent

JISTAN

TAJIKISTAN

Lanzhou

Xian

C H I N A

Hangzhou

Shanghai

Ryukyu Islands (Japan)

Tropic of Cancer

shkhabad

Dushanbe

Kabul

AFGHANISTAN

Islamabad

TIBET

Chengdu

Chongqing

Yangtse

Wuhan

East China Sea

P A C I F I C

Lhasa

Mekong

Taipei

TAIWAN

Lahore

NEPAL

BHUTAN

Thimphu

Kunming

Guangzhou

Shenzhen

PAKISTAN

Indus

Delhi

Katmandu

Cherrapunji

Hong Kong

O C E A N

Karachi

Ganges

BANGLADESH

Dacca

Hanoi

Luzon

Ahmadabad

Kolkata

BURMA (MYANMAR)

LAOS

Hainan

Manila

PHILIPPINES

I N D I A

Naypyidaw

Vientiane

Mumbai

Arabian Sea

Hyderabad

Rangoon

THAILAND

VIETNAM

CAMBODIA

South China Sea

Mindanao

Davao

Bangalore

Bay of Bengal

Bangkok

Phnom Penh

Ho Chi Minh City

Palawan

Chennai

Andaman Islands (India)

Bandar Seri Begawan

BRUNEI

Halmahera

Papua

Equator

Laccadive Islands (India)

Nicobar Islands (India)

SRI LANKA

MALAYSIA

Borneo

Celebes

Ceram

N E S I A

Colombo

Male

MALDIVES

North

Kuala Lumpur

SINGAPORE

Banjarmasin

Makassar

Arafura Sea

Palembang

I N D O

W E N S

I N D I A N   O C E A N

Jakarta

Java

Java Sea

Bali

Flores

Timor

Dili

EAST TIMOR

AUSTRALIA

East from Greenwich

COPYRIGHT PHILIP'S

# Africa

- *Africa is the second largest continent. Asia is the largest.*
- *There are over 50 countries, some of them small in area and population. The population of Africa is growing more quickly than any other continent.*
- *Parts of Africa have a dry, desert climate. Other parts are tropical.*
- *The highest mountains run from north to south on the eastern side of Africa. The Great Rift Valley is a volcanic valley that was formed 10 to 20 million years ago by a crack in the Earth's crust. Mount Kenya and Kilimanjaro are examples of old volcanoes in the area.*
- *The Sahara is the largest desert in the world.*

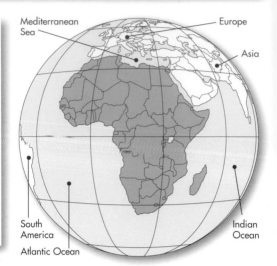

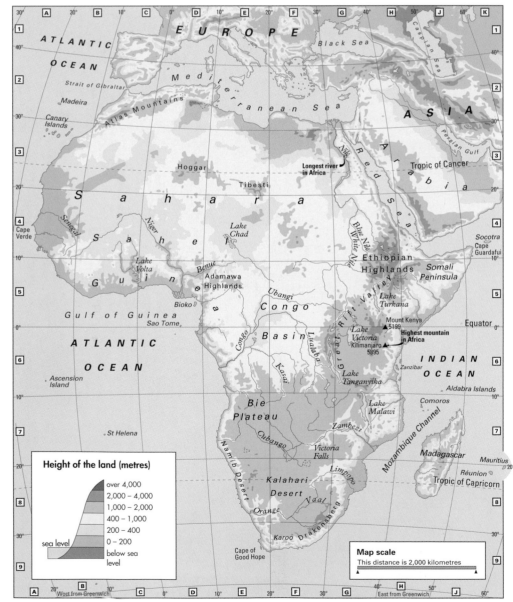

## Largest countries – by area

(thousand square kilometres)

| | |
|---|---|
| 1. Algeria | 2,382 |
| 2. Congo (Dem. Rep.) | 2,345 |
| 3. Sudan | 1,886 |
| 4. Libya | 1,760 |
| 5. Chad | 1,284 |
| 6. Niger | 1,267 |

## Largest countries – by population

(million people)

| | |
|---|---|
| 1. Nigeria | 170 |
| 2. Ethiopia | 94 |
| 3. Egypt | 84 |
| 4. Congo (Dem. Rep.) | 74 |
| 5. South Africa | 49 |
| 6. Tanzania | 47 |

## Largest cities

(million people)

| | |
|---|---|
| 1. Lagos (NIGERIA) | 11.2 |
| 2. Cairo (EGYPT) | 11.1 |
| 3. Kinshasa (CONGO, D. R.) | 8.8 |
| 4. Khartoum (SUDAN) | 5.1 |
| 5. Luanda (ANGOLA) | 5.1 |

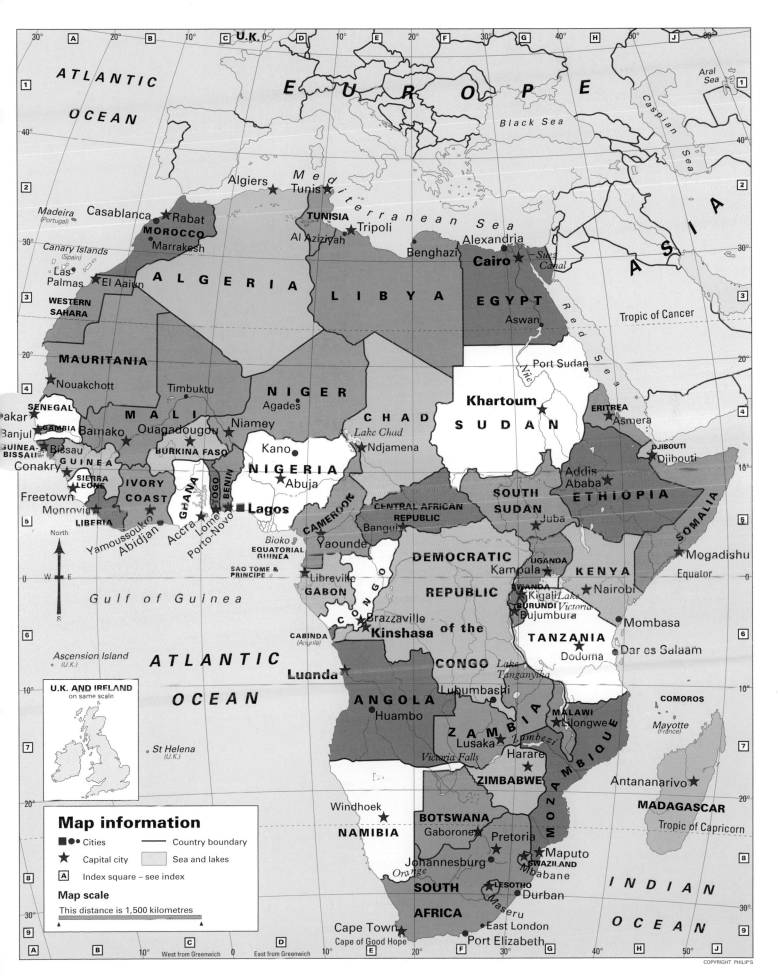

ATLANTIC
OCEAN

EUROPE

ASIA

Black Sea

Caspian Sea

Aral Sea

Madeira
(Portugal)

Algiers
Tunis

Mediterranean Sea

Casablanca
Rabat
MOROCCO
Marrakesh

TUNISIA
Al Aziziyah
Tripoli

Benghazi

Alexandria

Cairo
Suez Canal

Canary Islands
(Spain)

Las
Palmas

El Aaiun

ALGERIA

LIBYA

EGYPT

Aswan

Red Sea

Tropic of Cancer

WESTERN
SAHARA

MAURITANIA

Nouakchott

Timbuktu

NIGER

Agades

CHAD

Port Sudan

Nile

Khartoum

SUDAN

ERITREA

Asmera

SENEGAL

akar

Banjul

GAMBIA

GUINEA-
BISSAU

Bissau

Conakry

GUINEA

SIERRA
LEONE

Freetown

Monrovia

LIBERIA

MALI

Bamako

Ouagadougou

BURKINA FASO

Niamey

Kano

NIGERIA

Abuja

Lake Chad

Ndjamena

Lagos

CAMEROON

CENTRAL AFRICAN
REPUBLIC

Bangui

SOUTH
SUDAN

Juba

DJIBOUTI

Djibouti

Addis
Ababa

ETHIOPIA

SOMALIA

IVORY
COAST

GHANA

TOGO

BENIN

Yamoussoukro

Abidjan

Accra

Lome

Porto-Novo

Bioko

EQUATORIAL
GUINEA

SAO TOME &
PRINCIPE

Libreville

GABON

CONGO

Yaounde

DEMOCRATIC

REPUBLIC

of the

CONGO

UGANDA

Kampala

Kigali

RWANDA

BURUNDI

Bujumbura

Lake
Victoria

KENYA

Nairobi

Mogadishu

Equator

North

W E

S

Gulf of Guinea

ATLANTIC

OCEAN

Ascension Island
(U.K.)

U.K. AND IRELAND
on same scale

St Helena
(U.K.)

Brazzaville

Kinshasa

CABINDA
(Angola)

Luanda

ANGOLA

Huambo

Lubumbashi

Lake
Tanganyika

TANZANIA

Dodoma

Mombasa

Dar es Salaam

COMOROS

Mayotte
(France)

MALAWI

Lilongwe

ZAMBIA

Lusaka

Zambezi

Victoria Falls

Harare

MOZAMBIQUE

Antananarivo

MADAGASCAR

Tropic of Capricorn

Windhoek

BOTSWANA

Gaborone

Pretoria

Maputo

SWAZILAND

Mbabane

ZIMBABWE

NAMIBIA

Johannesburg

Orange

SOUTH
AFRICA

LESOTHO

Maseru

Durban

East London

INDIAN

OCEAN

Cape Town

Cape of Good Hope

Port Elizabeth

## Map information

- ■ ●● Cities
- ★ Capital city
- A Index square – see index
- —— Country boundary
- Sea and lakes

### Map scale

This distance is 1,500 kilometres

U.K.

55

# Australia and Oceania

- *The continent is often called Oceania. It is made up of the huge island of Australia and thousands of smaller islands in the Pacific Ocean.*

- *It is the smallest continent, only about a sixth the size of Asia.*

- *The highest mountain is on the Indonesian part of New Guinea which many consider to be part of Asia.*

## Largest countries – by area
### (thousand square kilometres)

| | |
|---|---|
| 1. Australia | 7,741 |
| 2. Papua New Guinea | 463 |
| 3. New Zealand | 271 |

## Largest countries – by population
### (million people)

| | |
|---|---|
| 1. Australia | 22 |
| 2. Papua New Guinea | 6 |

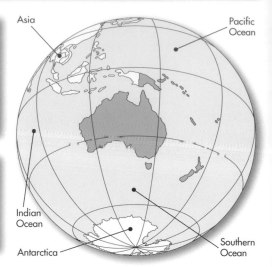

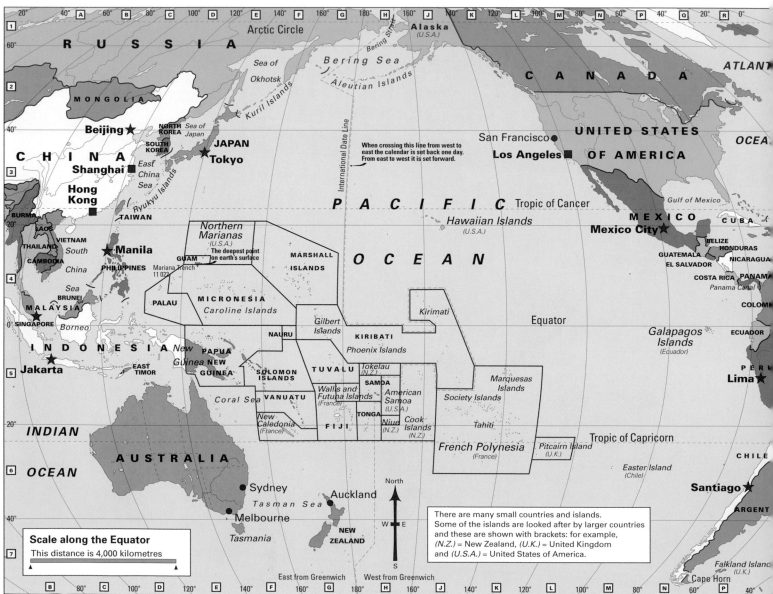

There are many small countries and islands. Some of the islands are looked after by larger countries and these are shown with brackets: for example, (N.Z.) = New Zealand, (U.K.) = United Kingdom and (U.S.A.) = United States of America.

Scale along the Equator
This distance is 4,000 kilometres

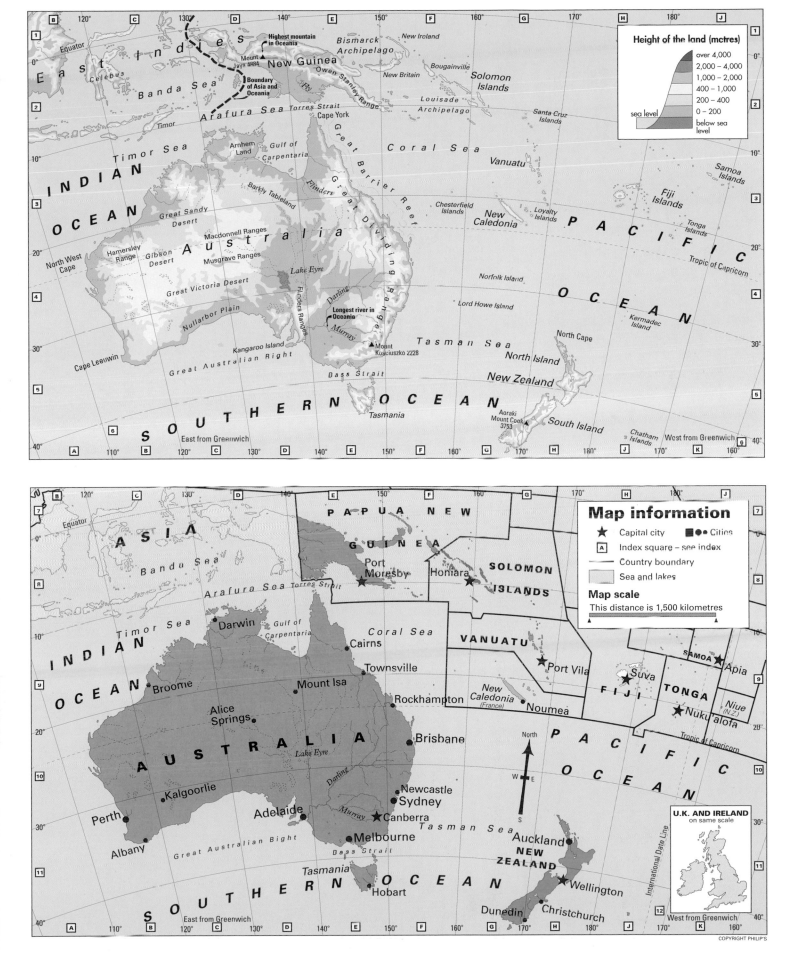

# North America

- North America is the third largest continent. It is half the size of Asia. It stretches almost from the Equator to the North Pole.

- Three countries – Canada, the United States and Mexico – make up most of the continent.

- Greenland, the largest island in the world, is included within North America.

- In the east there are a series of large lakes. These are called the Great Lakes. A large waterfall called Niagara Falls is between Lake Erie and Lake Ontario. The St Lawrence River connects the Great Lakes with the Atlantic Ocean.

- North and South America are joined by a narrow strip of land called the Isthmus of Panama.

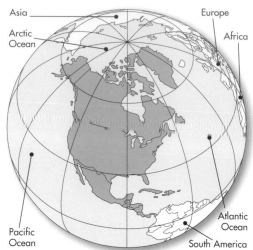

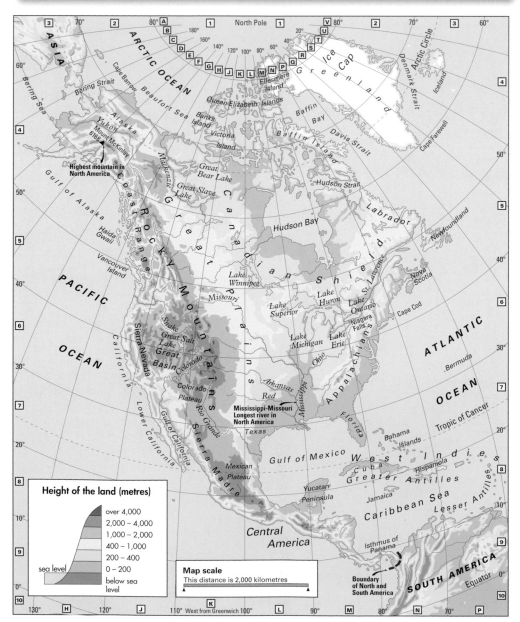

## Largest countries – by area

*(thousand square kilometres)*

| | | |
|---|---|---|
| 1. Canada | ........... | 9,971 |
| 2. United States | ...... | 9,629 |
| 3. Greenland | ........ | 2,176 |
| 4. Mexico | ........... | 1,958 |
| 5. Nicaragua | ......... | 130 |
| 6. Honduras | ......... | 112 |

## Largest countries – by population

*(million people)*

| | | |
|---|---|---|
| 1. United States | ....... | 314 |
| 2. Mexico | ........... | 115 |
| 3. Canada | ........... | 34 |
| 4. Guatemala | ......... | 14 |
| 5. Cuba | ........... | 11 |
| 6. Dominican Republic | .... | 10 |

## Largest cities

*(million people)*

| | | |
|---|---|---|
| 1. Mexico City (MEXICO) | .. | 20.4 |
| 2. New York (USA) | ..... | 19.4 |
| 3. Los Angeles (USA) | .... | 12.9 |
| 4. Chicago (USA) | ....... | 9.5 |
| 5. Dallas (USA) | ......... | 6.5 |

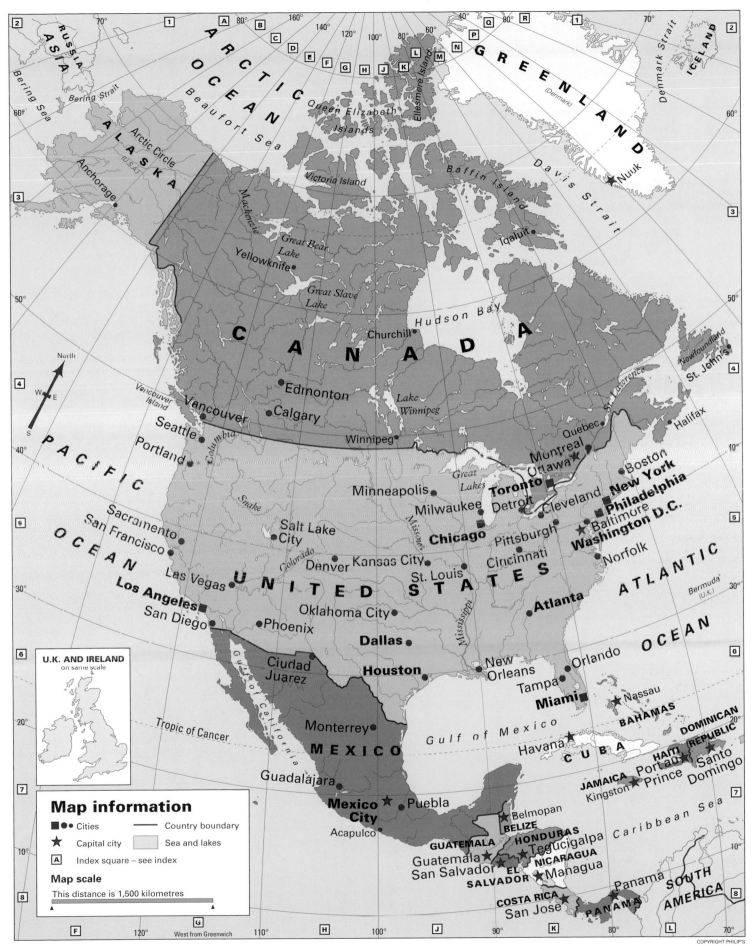

**Map information**

- ■●● Cities
- ★ Capital city
- Ⓐ Index square – see index
- —— Country boundary
- Sea and lakes

**Map scale**

This distance is 1,500 kilometres

U.K. AND IRELAND on same scale

COPYRIGHT PHILIP'S

# South America

- The Amazon is the second longest river in the world. The Nile is the longest river, but more water flows from the Amazon into the ocean than from any other river.

- The range of mountains called the Andes runs for over 7,500 km from north to south on the western side of the continent. There are many volcanoes in the Andes.

- Lake Titicaca is the largest lake in the continent. It has an area of 8,300 sq km and is 3,800 metres above sea level.

- Spanish and Portuguese are the principal languages spoken in South America.

- Brazil is the largest country in area and population, and has the largest city.

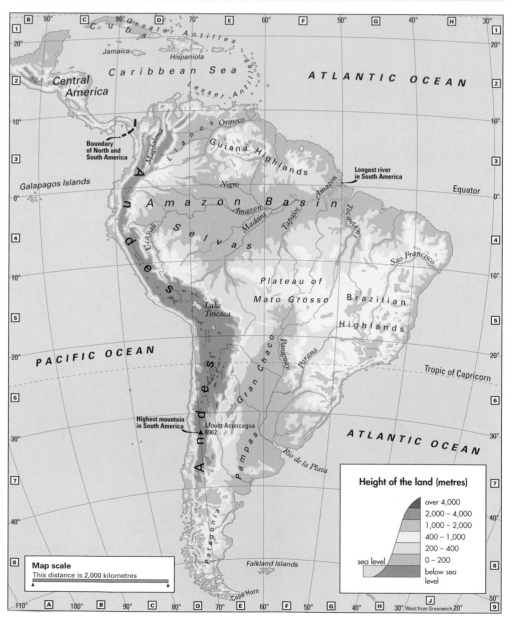

**Height of the land (metres)**

| | |
|---|---|
| | over 4,000 |
| | 2,000 – 4,000 |
| | 1,000 – 2,000 |
| | 400 – 1,000 |
| | 200 – 400 |
| sea level | 0 – 200 |
| | below sea level |

Map scale
This distance is 2,000 kilometres

## Largest countries – by area

(thousand square kilometres)

| | | |
|---|---|---|
| 1. | Brazil | 8,514 |
| 2. | Argentina | 2,780 |
| 3. | Peru | 1,285 |
| 4. | Colombia | 1,139 |
| 5. | Bolivia | 1,099 |
| 6. | Venezuela | 912 |

## Largest countries – by population

(million people)

| | | |
|---|---|---|
| 1. | Brazil | 206 |
| 2. | Colombia | 45 |
| 3. | Argentina | 42 |
| 4. | Peru | 30 |
| 5. | Venezuela | 28 |
| 6. | Chile | 17 |

## Largest cities

(million people)

| | | |
|---|---|---|
| 1. | Sao Paulo (BRAZIL) | 20.4 |
| 2. | Buenos Aires (ARGENTINA) | 13.5 |
| 3. | Rio de Janeiro (BRAZIL) | 12.0 |
| 4. | Lima (PERU) | 9.1 |
| 5. | Bogota (COLOMBIA) | 8.7 |

**B** 90° **C** 80° **D** 70° **E** 60° **F** 50° **G** 40° **H**

**1** BAHAMAS

CUBA

MEXICO

BELIZE JAMAICA HAITI DOMINICAN REPUBLIC PUERTO RICO (U.S.A.) VIRGIN ISLANDS (U.S.A.-U.K.)

**2** ST KITTS & NEVIS ANTIGUA & BARBUDA

GUATEMALA HONDURAS

*C a r i b b e a n   S e a*

GUADELOUPE (France) DOMINICA MARTINIQUE (France) ST LUCIA

EL SALVADOR NICARAGUA

ST VINCENT BARBADOS GRENADA

*ATLANTIC*

COSTA RICA

Barranquilla

CURACAO (Netherlands)

Caracas

Port of Spain TRINIDAD & TOBAGO

*OCEAN*

Panama Canal

Maracaibo

Valencia

*Orinoco*

PANAMA

VENEZUELA

Georgetown Paramaribo Cayenne

Medellin

Bogota

GUYANA SURINAME FRENCH GUIANA (France)

**3** COLOMBIA

Cali

*Negro*

*Amazon*

Equator

Quito

ECUADOR

Belem Sao Luis

Fortaleza

**4** Galapagos Islands (Ecuador)

Guayaquil

Iquitos

Manaus

*Madeira* *Tapajos*

B R A Z I L

Natal Joao Pessoa

Chiclayo

*Ucayali*

Recife

Trujillo

*Xingu* *Tocantins*

Maceio

PERU

*Sao Francisco*

Lima

Cusco

Salvador

**5** PACIFIC

Arequipa

*Lake Titicaca*

La Paz

Cuiaba

Brasilia

Sucre

BOLIVIA

Goiania

Belo Horizonte

**6** OCEAN

Antofagasta

PARAGUAY

*Parana*

Vitoria

Tropic of Capricorn

Asuncion

Campinas

Rio de Janeiro Sao Paulo

Tucuman

CHILE

Florianopolis

Curitiba

North

Porto Alegre

*ATLANTIC*

**7** Juan Fernandez (Chile)

Valparaiso

Cordoba

Rosario

URUGUAY

W E

Santiago

Buenos Aires

Montevideo

*OCEAN*

S

*Rio de la Plata*

Concepcion

ARGENTINA

**7** U.K. AND IRELAND on same scale

Bahia Blanca

**Map information**

■ ● • Cities ─── Country boundary

★ Capital city ▓ Sea and lakes

Ⓐ Index square – see index

**8**

Falkland Islands (U.K.) Stanley

**Map scale**

This distance is 1,500 kilometres

▲ ▲

South Georgia (U.K.)

**9** 50°

Punta Arenas

Cape Horn

**A** 100° **B** 90° **C** 80° **D** 70° **E** 60° **F** 50° **G** 40° **H** 30° **J** 20°

COPYRIGHT PHILIP'S

61

# Polar Regions

The Polar Regions are the areas around the North Pole and the South Pole. The area around the North Pole is called the **Arctic** and the area around the South Pole is called the **Antarctic**. The sun never shines straight down on the Arctic or Antarctic so they are very cold – the coldest places on Earth. The Arctic consists of frozen water. Some parts of Northern Europe, North America and Asia are inside the Arctic Circle. A group of people called the Inuit live there.

**Map information**

- Cities and towns
★ Capital cities
○ (Japan) Scientific stations in the Antarctic

Cross-section

Land covered in ice

Ice always in the sea

Ice sometimes in the sea

**Map scale**

This distance is 1,500 kilometres

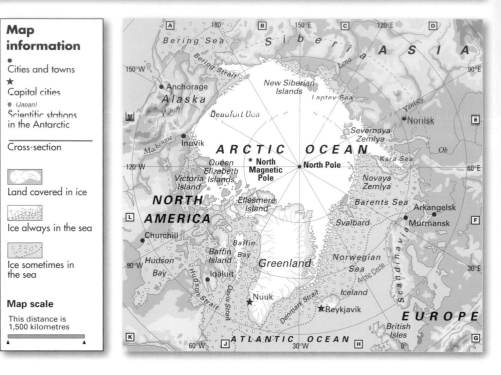

The Antarctic is a continent. It is bigger than Europe or Australia and has no permanent population. Most of the land consists of ice which is thousands of metres thick. At the edges, chunks of ice break off to make icebergs. These float out to sea. The diagram below shows a cross-section through Antarctica between two of the camps, Union Glacier Camp and Casey Station. It shows how thick the ice is on the ice sheets.

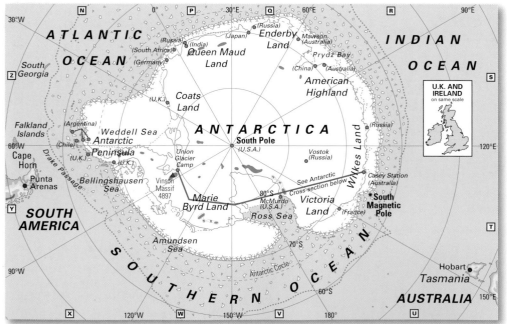

## Cross-section of the Antarctic

| | | | |
|---|---|---|---|
| 2,000 m | Transantarctic Mountains | East Antarctic Ice Sheet | 2,000 m |
| 1,000 m — Union Glacier Camp | I C E | I C E | Casey Station — 1,000 m |
| Weddell Sea sea level | West Antarctic Ice Sheet | Ross Ice Shelf | Indian Ocean sea level |
| −1,000 m | | | −1,000 m |
| −2,000 m | | | −2,000 m |
| | R O C K | R O C K | |

1,000 km 2,000 km 3,000 km 4,000 km 5,000 km 6,000 km

# Finding places

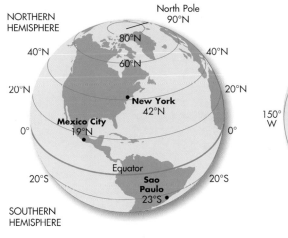

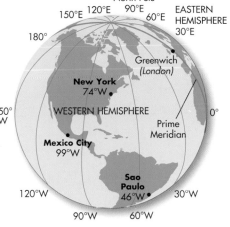

## Latitude

These three maps show part of the Earth as if seen from thousands of kilometres above New York. Exactly halfway between the North and South Poles is an imaginary line called the Equator. It divides the Earth into north and south hemispheres and is numbered 0°. On either side of the Equator run parallel lines called lines of latitude.

## Longitude

Maps have another set of lines running north to south linking the Poles. These lines are called lines of longitude. The line numbered 0° runs through Greenwich in London, England, and is called the Prime Meridian. The other lines of longitude are numbered up to 180° east and west of 0°. Longitude line 180° runs through the Pacific Ocean.

## Map references

The latitude and longitude lines on maps form a grid. In this atlas, the grid lines are in blue, and on most maps are shown for every ten degrees. The numbers of the lines can be used to give a reference to show the location of a place on a map. The index in this atlas uses another way of finding places. It lists the rows of latitude as numbers and the columns of longitude as letters.

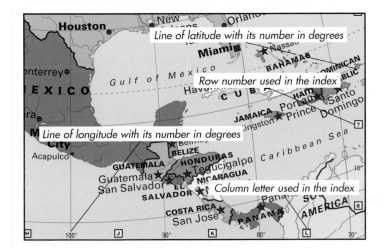

Line of latitude with its number in degrees

Row number used in the index

Line of longitude with its number in degrees

Column letter used in the index

| | Latitude | Longitude | Map page | Map letter-number |
|---|---|---|---|---|
| Lagos, Africa | 6°N | 3°E | 55 | D5 |
| Mexico City, North America | 19°N | 99°W | 59 | H7 |
| Moscow, Europe | 55°N | 37°E | 51 | Q4 |
| Sao Paulo, South America | 23°S | 46°W | 61 | G6 |
| Sydney, Oceania | 34°S | 151°E | 57 | F11 |
| Tokyo, Asia | 35°N | 139°E | 53 | R5 |

*This table shows the largest city in each continent with its latitude and longitude. Look for them on the maps in this atlas using the letter-number references.*

# Index of place names

The names in the index are in alphabetical order. To find a place on a map in the atlas, first find the name in the index. The first number after the place name is the map page number. After the page number there is a letter and another number. The **letter** shows you the **column** where the place is on the map and the **number** shows you the **row**. If the place name goes across more than one square, the reference is to the square where the name begins.